THE
PROMISE
OF
PARADISE

ALSO BY JONATHAN H. ELLERBY, Ph.D.

*GODWORKS: Why God Is Nothing You'd Expect
and Everything You Need* (e-book)

*INSPIRATION DEFICIT DISORDER:
The No-Pill Prescription to End High Stress,
Low Energy, and Bad Habits**

*RETURN TO THE SACRED:
Pathways to Spiritual Awakening**

WORKING WITH INDIGENOUS ELDERS

*YOUR SPIRITUAL PERSONALITY:
Finding the Path That's Right for You* (CD)

*Available from Hay House

Please visit:

Hay House USA: **www.hayhouse.com**®
Hay House Australia: **www.hayhouse.com.au**
Hay House UK: **www.hayhouse.co.uk**
Hay House South Africa: **www.hayhouse.co.za**
Hay House India: **www.hayhouse.co.in**

THE
PROMISE
OF
PARADISE

LIFE-CHANGING LESSONS
FROM THE TROPICS

Jonathan H. Ellerby, Ph.D.

HAY HOUSE, INC.
Carlsbad, California • New York City
London • Sydney • Johannesburg
Vancouver • Hong Kong • New Delhi

Published and distributed in the United States by: Hay House, Inc.: www
.hayhouse.com® • **Published and distributed in Australia by:** Hay House
Australia Pty. Ltd.: www.hayhouse.com.au • **Published and distributed
in the United Kingdom by:** Hay House UK, Ltd.: www.hayhouse.co.uk •
Published and distributed in the Republic of South Africa by: Hay House
SA (Pty), Ltd.: www.hayhouse.co.za • **Distributed in Canada by:** Raincoast:
www.raincoast.com • **Published in India by:** Hay House Publishers India:
www.hayhouse.co.in

Interior design: Nick C. Welch

Library of Congress Cataloging-in-Publication Data

Ellerby, Jonathan H.
The promise of paradise : life-changing lessons from the tropics / Jonathan H.
Ellerby. -- 1st ed.
    p. cm.
  ISBN 978-1-4019-3959-5 (pbk. : alk. paper) 1. Contentment. 2. Simplicity. 3.
Lifestyles--Psychological aspects. 4. Conduct of life. I. Title.
   BJ1533.C7E45 2012
   204.092--dc23
   [B]
                                                            2011044613

ISBN: 978-1-4019-3959-5
Digital ISBN: 978-1-4019-3960-1
Gift Edition ISBN: 978-1-4019-4013-3

15 14 13 12   4 3 2 1
1st edition, February 2012

Printed in the United States of America

*For Benjamin, in honor of your
vision and friendship.*

CONTENTS

Foreword by Benjamin Beja ix

Chapter 1: Have You Lost Your Mind?.............................. 1

Chapter 2: A Red Car and Other Stuff............................ 19

Chapter 3: A Kiss on the Cheek 35

Chapter 4: Sunburn and Snorkeling 49

Chapter 5: Catch of the Day 61

Chapter 6: Head in the Sand.. 75

Chapter 7: A Goat in the Backseat of a Volkswagen........ 87

Chapter 8: Beauty Everywhere... 99

Chapter 9: The Call and the Commitment 117

An Exercise to Help You Get Started: What Inspires You? 135

Learn More 139

Acknowledgments 140

About the Author 142

FOREWORD

When I was very young I loved to travel. I started traveling in my homeland of Mexico, but by the time I was in my 30s, I had traveled all over the world. At first, I liked to visit and live in major cities. The amazing architecture, the diverse cultures, and the race of progress was impressive to me. It wasn't long before that experience began to lose its luster and I became very interested in visiting smaller towns and villages.

My main motivation for travel was always curiosity: learning about other countries, people, and traditions. For me it wasn't enough to read about different ways in the world; I wanted to experience them. Naturally, my attention went to observing and exploring our similarities and our differences as people of various cultures and regions. As I went further into this process, over time I realized that the major differences I could see were not cultural. I saw that our differences had everything to do with the size of the city people lived in and its growth—and not so much to the country, culture, or traditions.

I started to see that the major change humankind has passed through in the last 200 years has been due to the growth of populations and places. Villages became cities or fell into hardship, smaller cities became major metropolises, and new cities were created.

The strong migration pattern of people from rural areas to urban areas and the future trends are mind-blowing; in the next 35 years, 3.5 billion people will migrate to or will be born in a major city. That means that the majority of the world will live in a city, along with a high concentration of people.

Even though the positive aspect of this growth is about accommodating the daily needs of the more than 7 billion people in the world, the cost has been enormous in areas such as the environment, income disparity, regional conflicts, sustainability, and family disintegration. Worse, our major cities have devastated people's sense of belonging, general happiness, connection, and the chance to live simply.

I envision that in the next 50 to 100 years, we will keep seeing amazing changes in the way we live and how we relate to others. The learning, technology, wealth, and consciousness we have achieved are unparalleled by any other time in human history. It is impressive and hard to imagine where we are heading. At the same time, the need for smaller communities will grow, and the desire for more meaningful experiences of community and connection will become a desperate issue.

When considering the source of future change, I see the deepest and most meaningful changes happening at the community level and not at an institutional level (government, schools, religious institutions, and the like)—they will be too busy reinventing themselves. The major change is going to happen in how we connect with other human beings in meaningful and deeper ways, identify with our group and groups related to us, and achieve a strong sense of belonging and ultimately live a happier and more inspired life.

When I met Jonathan Ellerby, I knew that he was exactly the type of teacher, healer, and corporate visionary that our new world will need. Since Jonathan became the Tao Inspired Living CEO, we have made great strides toward becoming a wellness company of the future, one where heart and soul are as essential as profit or growth. So much of the magic and wisdom that Jonathan offers is found here in this book. It's the simplest of anything he has written, maybe deceivingly simple. In these pages you will experience and sense the power of courageous change and how you can take such steps. You catch a glimpse of the beauty of our region, and why Jonathan, myself, and our team of talented people are working to create more than inspired events and programs for people to visit, but an extraordinary place to live.

The Promise of Paradise is a book that is about taking risks, finding what you love, and learning how to make it all happen. It is also Jonathan's story of what he risked to join Tao as our CEO. From the moment we met, I could see that we were committed to similar missions and the common belief that what the world needs now is more meaningful connections, not less. Tao Inspired Living is committed to building communities that matter and make a difference. This is how we seek to change the world: by fostering communities that are all about creating meaningful relationships among their members, with a strong sense of belonging, and a shared commitment to making themselves and the world better. We have built a place where individuals from all over the world can connect, reinvigorate, belong, and live their own dreams.

In the Riviera Maya, we have learned that paradise is not just in where you live, but *how* you live. This inspiring book will help you explore some of the most important questions of your life, in a fun and straightforward way. We invite you to take a look and find out if our vision inspires yours.

— **Benjamin Beja**
Founder, Tao Inspired Living
Riviera Maya, 2012

Chapter One

HAVE YOU LOST
YOUR MIND?

How Do You Start Your Day?

It is early on a Sunday morning. My wife and son are still asleep, and I have perched myself like a seagull on our small balcony overlooking the Caribbean Sea. Watching, waiting, breathing in the deep sea air, I am still half asleep but eager for what is about to happen. Morning birds and lizards animate the green canopy of trees below. An explosion of butterflies and the warm wind add to the magic of the moment. The sun is still absent, and the sea is a dark, surging blue in the shadow of the curve of the earth. Soon all that will change. And then, it begins. The first rays of light shine from the watery horizon, and carefully the sun begins to rise, emerging in the distance like a radiant sphere of diamond light.

Here the sunrise can be so intense that it's almost impossible to look at. The sky and sea around it are burned into an amazing, brilliant, golden white light that my eyes can barely withstand. I look anyway. Breathing deeply, receiving more than searching, as if somewhere in that radiance I might catch a glimpse of God or Nirvana. . . .

And I do.

In that moment everything in my world is all right again, and there is nothing left to do or become.

It's not a bad way to start the day.

There is no doubt in my heart or mind that I am living in the right place, that I am exactly where I am meant to be. I have found, or co-created you might say, my own paradise. It is amazing and hard to believe at times. Yet paradise didn't come easily. Extraordinary gifts usually come at an extraordinary price. Risk is often a key to the formula. Living in the tropical wonderland of the Riviera Maya, Mexico, is a dream come true for me. It required, however, that my family and I give up a different dream first—one that others may have held for us; one that many people would find impossible to let go of. Our journey into this paradise was complete with deep sacrifice, embracing the unknown, and the mythic voices of our society that attempted to keep us "safe" and where life could continue as usual. Finding your paradise is not about doing what is typical. Paradise has always been guarded by the fiery swords of doubt and convention. Even the ancient scriptures tell us so.

Despite the fear and media scares about a lawless country of drug lords and violence, we have seen nothing of the kind in our Mexican Eden. Here we live far from the U.S. border towns that are making the daily headlines. Here we live where it's hard not to run into people you know and like, among the villages, cities, and hotels that are strung like glittering beads on the white sand beaches that line our precious coast. Here people are forgiving and strangers are quick to help. It is not difficult to feel accepted and safe—if you allow it.

These days when I visit the U.S. and see the fearful news about Mexico, I am reminded of when I traveled in and around the Middle East. I recall that in such places many people were flooded with images and ideas of the materialistic, Godless, oversexed, gun- and power-obsessed Americans. Of course that too is a story that simply is not entirely true. I lived in the United States for most of my adult life and found so many American people to be mostly the opposite of their overseas stereotypes. Resting in the light of a quiet morning by the sea, it's hard to believe the world is so full of fear and generalizations. Sometimes it makes me laugh. My wife, Monica, and I have never lived in a place where we felt so safe, where people were so easy to relate to, or where we were so easily connected to our community. I try to keep myself present to what is true around me, and not so much the stories I hear about it. It helps to be an observer. It helps to release the impulse to jump to conclusions.

Later in the morning, we ride our bikes to the local farmers' market. We take our time to press through the morning humidity, down the bumpy hand-built road in the sleepy seaside Caribbean town of Akumal, our son towing behind in the bike carriage we brought from Arizona. We watch for the familiar faces of the locals and the interesting display of tourists. Our boy watches for wildlife: iguanas, coatis, stray dogs, and raccoons. Our pace is easy; we aren't in a rush. Taking our time is our goal, and enjoying each other is the measure of a successful day. Our errands will be accomplished, but Life, people, and health will not be put aside for ambition.

I remember Sunday mornings back in Tucson—they were also wonderful. Sometimes I would hop into the car to grab a few things at our local grocery store before a big weekend breakfast. We took our time there also, yet, somehow, it wasn't the same. We had to drive everywhere and few of our local shop owners remembered us from one visit to another. Shopping was a big part of life. It seemed that the world around us wanted us to play a game that we just didn't understand or enjoy. Time in the backyard often led to time at the hardware store and garden center; and time away from home often meant time at an event, which meant souvenirs and admission fees; and time at home often meant an awareness of all the things we wanted to fix, replace, and buy. It was a beautiful life, but something was missing. Too often we thought the missing piece was at a local store or a function of our income level, no matter how much it grew.

The Teacher Must Also Be the Student

My story of transformation is both typical and extraordinary. People who have read my other books know that my training and life experience have been anything but ordinary. From studying at the side of African shamans in remote villages to advising executives in multinational companies like PepsiCo, I have roamed the worlds of health, healing, leadership, and spirituality in many forms and vehicles. But being a senior executive of organizational change in a major health-care network and an apprentice to a Native American healer for much of my adult life did not completely prepare me for the everyday challenges of marriage and raising a child.

Completing a Ph.D. in comparative religion, working as a hospital chaplain, and leading the spiritual program department for one of the world's most famous health resorts didn't help me protect my home from foreclosure in a free-falling economy. Being a counselor and coach to some of the world's most powerful celebrities and CEOs did not protect me from becoming disconnected from my own health practices when the pressures of success and change began to mount. These experiences only confirmed the lesson: no matter what you have or who you think you are, if you engage life fully, you will not be fully immune to the stresses and distresses of Life. Money doesn't equal happiness, power doesn't equal peace of mind, and profound mystical experiences are not a hall pass to skip the hard lessons of life. It sounds good, but if you have a family, career success, and a mortgage, think again. Such earthly delights will be your greatest blessings and your greatest tests.

The irony in my story, of course, is that my big inspiration and desire for change came to me while I was helping other people find the very same experience. Just when I felt I was on the "right" track helping others make their dreams come true, I was handed a new dream—or you might say that I saw through the illusions of the old one. It happened very quickly for me. If you are fearless in the face of change and willing to listen and look for the cues, a profound transformation can come quickly for you, too.

In the summer of 2010 my book *Inspiration Deficit Disorder: The No-Pill Prescription to End High Stress, Low Energy, and Bad Habits* was published. It wasn't a runaway hit, but it did very well and made it on a few little-known bestseller lists. The topic of managing stress, breaking bad habits, and finding your passions shot me into more mainstream media, including daytime network TV and top-tier magazines such as *Ladies' Home Journal, Reader's Digest,* and *Woman's Day.* So many gifts and opportunities flowed from the book's release, and I was overwhelmed by my own sense of gratitude for all that I had in life. Everything appeared to be on track.

I had only blessings to count. I was blessed with a wonderful wife and son, a beautiful home in an incredible city that I loved, and a steady job as the Spiritual Program Director for the famous Canyon Ranch Health Resorts. My book career was clearly underway with Hay House, one of the largest publishers of personal growth.

TV spots were getting easier to secure, and my appearance on *Larry King Live* was a springboard for new media opportunities. My consulting clients, which included the government of Canada, were strong and steady. I was even working on a TV show concept with United Talent Agency, one of the three biggest talent agencies in the world. What more could I ask for? Was it really a dream come true?

Despite my success, it all came with one major problem for me: the greatest liability of writing personal-growth and life-improvement books is that you often find yourself not only consumed by the topic you are writing about, but also that Life actually conspires to force you to live the lessons you are teaching. In short, you must practice what you preach—or face great costs! I know of an author who wrote about how to avoid divorce, and prior to his book's publication, his marriage fell apart. I also know a spiritual teacher who taught people how to build community, yet he unconsciously tore his own apart.

We have all heard of individuals who claim to show us how to become wealthy and invincible, and yet they often end up broken, poor, or even in jail. So many sad, ironic stories behind the scenes of those who teach people how to cope and then are faced with the test of their teachings. There is an old saying: "Those who know do not teach; those who teach do not know." It's a hard lesson for someone who feels born to teach, but a worthy warning for us all.

A Professional Liability

I suppose I had forgotten about that strange law of nature when I decided to write a book about stress, bad habits, and disconnection in order to help people create an inspired life. Regardless of all the external successes, the period of time that followed the completion and release of the book was one of the most stressful in my life, and it led to the breaking of many of my own healthy habits. There were also health problems in my home that stretched and tested my relationship with my wife. The increasing scope of my work meant I was taking on bigger and bigger business costs and a growing debt, while the overwhelming demand for my attention came at the cost of my own well-being because I refused to let it take time away from my son and wife. I, like too many, was convinced I could sacrifice myself and place my family first and my career closely second. There was never enough time. Something had to give. It was just too many things, even if most of them were a "dream come true."

Remember that stress is a response to change, challenge, demand, and attention. It is not always about "bad" situations; it's often about the volume, pace, and nature of your situations. And so, "Dr. Create-an-Inspired-Life" became overwhelmed by a haunting feeling that he (I) might not be headed in the right direction. When I spoke about inspiration, I repeatedly asked the audience, "Are you living your most inspired life?" Again and again I asked people to look deeper and be honest: "Is this really your best life?" And like a magic spell, the question began to echo in my own mind. *Am I living my most inspired life? My best life?*

Against all logic, I began to question my work and the path ahead. I knew that if I was asking other people to look twice at their situation and really take risks to design an extraordinary life, then I had to do the same. Even though I had created a life that I loved, I needed to carefully examine if it was still true for me. Was I still in love with what I was creating? Was I inspired, or just inspiring others? Often it is harder to create change when all is well rather than when all is lost. People who are in deep struggle are typically motivated by their pain and discomfort to aspire and grow. Those who are comfortable in a life that simply no longer fits typically lack the incentive to create change. Most people who knew me at the time felt that I was making all the right moves and was positioned for a steady rise.

But I had to ask: a steady rise to what?

I have always taught my clients that in life we must learn to love the journey and the process, because dreams and goals will always remain in the ever-shifting future. Inspiration is not an end point; it's a way of living each moment. It is a process of listening and refining and redirecting. True inspiration is dynamic and can influence all areas of our lives for the better. One of the strangest things about inspiration is that it is never static—it always evolves and grows.

Just when you think you've reached your peak, you find a new one, or maybe realize your next goal is to have no peaks! Inspiration should come with a feeling of balance. If you love your job but it robs you of your relationships, then that is not an evolved inspiration. If you love your partner, but that love consumes and imbalances your life, that is *not* a genuine inspiration. Even if you've trusted your intuition and manifested the most inspired life you can imagine, it too must grow and change, or even an inspired life will become a golden cage.

In an effort to live what I teach, in the fall of 2010 I reviewed my life to find the growing sense that Spirit (name it what you like) was calling me to something new. I knew I had every blessing, and my American Dream was coming true. How could I ask for something more or different? I tried to avoid it, but it absolutely felt like Life wanted something different from me.

Each time I sat quietly or prayed deeply, I could sense a clear whisper within; I knew everything had to change. The more I listened, the more I felt it, and the more I knew I couldn't ignore it. If you listen to your heart long enough, eventually you will cross a threshold and the sheer force of the feeling that things must change will never let you be the same again. Sometimes the next step is clear and sometimes it's a leap of faith, either way it's a call that is dangerous to ignore. The cost of ignoring your true self and true calling is something I discuss at length in my book *Inspiration Deficit Disorder,* and I am convinced it is at the root of most health problems.

I was unsure of what was next. I knew that the path I was on seemed amazing to everyone who watched . . . although somehow, it was no longer amazing to me. It was no longer heading where my soul needed to go.

Cautious that it wasn't simply boredom or impatience, I realized that I had to take a leap of faith, a quantum leap. Everything was about to change.

I started to research new jobs, consider new projects, meet new people, and explore all my options. How would I make a jump from what I had to something I couldn't yet imagine? I decided to focus on the only thing I could do: I meditated more, I listened more, and I paid attention to my intuition. Slowly, images and ideas emerged like sea turtles rising toward the surface of the ocean. I would catch a glimpse, feel the excitement, and then, it would pass.

It didn't take much time to uncover what I was longing for in my heart of hearts: more time in nature; more time with my family; a life in a beautiful place near the ocean; and a job that would let me express my full creativity in a mission to spread a message of health, inspiration, and spirit in a real and meaningful way. I wanted to be in a community or culture where I felt challenged and affirmed, and I wanted my life to keep me at the edge of self-awareness: present, evolving, engaged.

But where—and how?

How Much Would You Give?

I soon faced the final test. It wasn't enough to consider changing jobs; this was a movement that felt much deeper and bigger than me and my wife. Something else had to make the decision, and I had to trust that. After much research into new options and a series of promising synchronicities, I knew that the only way to accelerate my leap forward was to cut ties with the past. I quit my job with nothing and nowhere to go next. It was wonderful work that I loved and excelled at, but it was no longer a fit. Waiting for what was next felt more and more false with each passing day, so with gratitude, I left.

I lined up some consulting work to get our family through the next month or two, but I had nothing fixed beyond that except for mounting bills from PR companies and costly travel expenses related to promoting my book. I immediately began to let people know of my new freedom and openness to change. At the back of my mind, there was one opportunity that I couldn't stop thinking about, but it was in Mexico and everyone around me was convinced that it wouldn't be a viable option. Life there couldn't possibly be better than the United States. No matter how great the project, relocating couldn't be good for my career and family. Or could it?

Just before I left my job, my family and I had visited the extraordinary region called the Riviera Maya, a 75-mile (more or less) stretch of white sand coast, lush jungle, and turquoise sea that accounts for over 70 percent of all of Mexico's tourist revenue. With the second-largest coral reef in the world, a network of ancient Mayan ruins, and endless outdoor adventures, it is easy to fall in love with. We had visited because of the invitation of a man, Benjamin Beja, whom I met by chance when I was a keynote speaker at a conference in the U.S.

Benjamin had told me of a wellness center and community that he had dreamed up and that he thought I might be a valuable consultant to the project. He didn't want to discuss a lot of details. "First," he insisted, "you need to come visit." The trip to Mexico was more wonderful than we expected, and when we left we could not imagine how we might return or for how long. Everyone we met there seemed to think they had found paradise, and we too thought that might be true.

Finally, Life made the biggest decision for us. One week after I quit my job, my wife and I were both offered work with Benjamin's amazing new project called "Tao," a sanctuary for wellness and healthy living that was being created between Akumal and Tulum, located in the heart of the Riviera Maya. We were invited to join as founders, creators, and partners. The money wasn't great to begin and the fear about moving to Mexico was distracting . . . but the opportunity for both of us was everything we wanted but couldn't put into words—a dream better and more wonderful than we could have conceived of in our suburban harbor.

One month later I accepted the position of CEO for the Tao Inspired Living, a new and growing wellness company—complete with plans for a wellness center and an Inspired Living residential community. The next three months were filled with difficult decisions, relationship stress, and the burden of trying to determine how we could transition all we had worked so hard to create to a place we barely knew 3,000 miles away. At the end of those three months, our home was for sale, three-quarters of our possessions were sold or in storage, and we were sitting on a beach in a place that can only be described as paradise.

Three Tropical Teachings

1. *Accept paradox.* Deep inspiration typically starts by creating massive imbalance and the feeling of total breakdown. Things often get worse before better. If it is true inspiration, however, it will eventually restore and create a new balance in your life.

2. *Be irrational.* The most important things in your life will defy logic. Powerful clarity comes from learning to listen to your intuition. What you need most is not always sensible or what you think it should be. The mind is a small part of true genius and a smaller part of knowing true peace. If everything in your life makes perfect "sense," something is probably missing.

3. *Choose courage.* Courage is essential in meaningful change. Inspired people take risks. If you aren't afraid when you make your next big change, your change is not big enough.

Chapter Two

A RED CAR AND OTHER STUFF

Many Splendid Things

My son, Narayan, celebrated his third birthday in Mexico. It was much more modest than his poolside *Go, Diego, Go!* themed second birthday back in Tucson, since party supplies and toys are simply harder to find and more expensive where we live now. My brother and his wife were visiting us at the time, and instead of seeking out a jumping castle or indoor playland (which *do* exist in this part of the world), we all went snorkeling in a local cenote—a stunning spring-fed pool of water in the jungle floor that opens into a large limestone cave in the earth. There are hundreds of cenotes in the region, each more spectacular than the next: radiant blue water; twisting caverns to swim through; and an unspeakable play of light between the reflections, shade, jungle, and open space. At three, Narayan has already learned to hold his breath and wear a snorkeling mask. For him, cenotes are a favorite. He loves to watch the vividly colored and strange-shaped fish that share the cenotes with locals and tourists. The underwater limestone formations are mysterious and magical, and I think that he, like myself and others, feels transported to a new universe when he enters one. It was as special a birthday as I can imagine.

Of course, toys are still a regular fixation for our boy, but much of his time is now spent playing with places, people, and ideas instead of things. His attention is most focused on the beach, in our community pool, or simply exploring the jungle-lined streets of our village. Occasionally he watches a video on a small portable player, but we haven't yet succumbed to watching much television nor do we have a TV. My son's world is now very different from the one I grew up in: the food, language, and enchanted landscape of the tropics have created a backdrop for his story with an impact I cannot yet imagine. In some ways I suppose he has less, and in other ways he has much, much more.

In contrast, I was born and raised in Winnipeg, a prairie town in the middle of Canada. Near to a maze of freshwater lakes and surrounded by expansive farming fields, Winnipeg is a somewhat small but progressive and self-assuredly metropolitan center, complete with a hockey team, football team, ballet, opera, and massive concert hall frequented by the likes of U2 and Coldplay.

Looking back, I think I was raised with very solid, humanistic, and humble values. My family didn't praise wealth or flashy things, and never cared too much for celebrity gossip. I didn't think we were overly attached to "things" and always knew that people came first. I certainly didn't think that wealth or possessions were a priority. I've spent much time in cities like New York and Los Angeles, as well as in the company of many clients who were more than millionaires. In these settings, I often witnessed the height of materialism and shallow greed, and I never thought of myself as materialistic by any of these standards. For extended periods, I have stayed in small African villages and Native American reservation towns. In many of my travels I have lived in some of the poorest conditions you can imagine . . . and I was always happy and felt like I had enough. Many of my spiritual experiences and lessons—which I described in my book *Return to The Sacred*—left me feeling liberated from the need for wealth or luxury. And so for all of my adult life I was convinced I had escaped the lure of materialism and was proud of it—until I moved to the Riviera Maya. Then I learned something else about myself, something that surprised me.

At the beginning of 2011, we were a two-car family. My wife and I worked in different directions in Tucson and had to trade off driving our son to preschool. We chose to live in a scenic part of town without public buses, so having two cars seemed logical and easy. Once faced with the big move to the Yucatán, it was clear that traveling nearly 3,000 miles with two cars and our entire household wasn't going to be easy to explain at the border, given that we had tourist status at the time and legally could only bring one car in. Our work visas were to be processed after we arrived, and we were faced with an impossible task: moving our home.

We could not take both cars (since we weren't about to drive a few thousand miles separately with a toddler), and as "tourists," we couldn't really haul a trailer or hire a van to tote all our stuff. If we did, it would be at an incredible and unaffordable cost. Whatever we could fit into one car is what would have to be acceptable for us in our new life. One car! This meant that none of the old rosewood Indian furniture we had collected could join us nor the flat-screen TV or the lawn furniture, no decorative bed pillows or large stereo system, no barbeque . . . none of it! The truth of my attachment to things began to be exposed.

We decided to sell our smaller cars for one massive juggernaut of an SUV. It was ideal: good on rough roads, able to carry at least a portion of our home, and was a brand and style that would not stand out in our new homeland. If we could only take one car's worth of things, we would make it the biggest car we could find!

I realize a person in my situation has *nothing* to complain about, but all suffering is relative; and when we realized we had to reduce all of our belongings to what we could cram into the back of an SUV, we were at a total loss. Our home compressed into a car? Were we crazy? Were we really about to give up everything we worked so hard to acquire?

At the time of our move, Monica and I had been married and living together for seven years with a house for five. We were pursuing the American Dream with a bohemian flare and had a beautiful home with a yard, a garage full of seasonal gear, and a thousand other things—and, of course, huge credit card debt. We had it all: Lights and decor for Christmas, Hanukkah, Halloween, and Easter. Camping gear to complete the summit of Everest. Enough art supplies for a small college. Tools and car parts for projects I'd never complete, much less understand. We had lots of *stuff!*

And none of this even begins to address the interior of our home. We were fortunate and worked very hard to create a beautiful, loving nest that even Martha Stewart —despite our differences in taste—would admire. With each anniversary, birthday, romantic celebration and near marital collapse, we would accumulate some new fixture or finishing to make our space just a little more perfect, just a little more "us."

Neither Monica nor I could see our accumulation of things objectively since it felt good, it felt right, and we could afford it. Everyone who visited us rewarded our addiction to home decor with deeply spiritual praise, such as, "There is such a special feeling here," or "Wow, I feel so much better when I visit your home—it is *so* healing," and even, "You've really created a sacred space." I look at our unconscious consumption and remember a wise saying: "You can never have enough of what you don't really need."

It all appeared wonderful in the moment, and it truly was a warm and beautiful home—and all that praise only confirmed that we were on the "right track."

It was very easy to fall into a form of spiritual material-ism until we had to decide which items of this global bazaar to pack into the back of a truck—and what to do with everything else. Then our sanctuary became more like a prison.

The Golden Cage

Here I was, a man who had lived without shelter, water, or food for days at a time; a man who had trav-eled the world with only a backpack . . . and yet, let-ting go of treasured CDs, books, and art? Impossible! These things were precious. They carried the memories of my travels and marked our marriage, our successes, and even our values. They'd become very important to me, and I didn't want to let them go. How could I? How would we live without them? It didn't seem fair.

What had happened? Was it a spell I was under? A marketing trick? How does a mystic like myself end up clinging to his DVD player and solar patio lights!? How did I get so attached to so much stuff?

By the time the day of our move arrived, we had reviewed every single object in our home: every photo, paper clip, crayon, AA battery . . . *everything.* It turned out to be an amazing and profound process. Cleaning out your closets and releasing things from the past will do as much as a few months of therapy for most people. On that last morning before our move, not only had we evaluated, sold, packed, or given away all our things, but we had also reached a new place in our selves. We weren't just letting go of things; we were renewing old stories, releasing old burdens, and becoming free.

It was a function of running out of time and space, but the result was a true release, a true awakening. Things we could not imagine living without in February, we were easily and willingly giving away in April. The belongings that used to feel like a comfort had become a stress and a burden.

By the time we were ready to pack the car, we were ready to leave *everything* behind. And when we crossed that line, that moment, the stress faded. The lesson was crystal clear: *things* just didn't matter that much, and attachment to them is more trouble than it is worth. We were becoming free from our consumer-driven lives, and it felt good. Maybe living simply wasn't a design statement or even about buying the "right" things with the right values; maybe it was about having *less* and being okay with that. It turns out I was much more attached to things than I had thought.

If you ever think you are free of something—drugs, alcohol, fatty foods, bad relationships, whatever—try living without it. I have counseled hundreds of people who have told me they were "done" with drinking, even though they still drank; or "done" with an ex-partner, even though they still had sex with him or her; or "done" with ambition, even though they still worked endless hours at the expense of their health. It's the age-old claim, "I can quit whenever I want to," or "I don't need it; I just choose to do it, but I can stop any time." If you believe that is true, test it. We did.

After we were settled in our new home for a month, it became clear that we could live without all we had and that a simpler life was also a better life for us. On the other hand, we were faced with an unavoidable consumer need: a second car. Only then did we realize how deeply the roots of our consumer mentality ran.

Just a Car?

Where we live in Mexico, a car is a luxury that most people cannot afford, and a second car is a major indulgence, which the majority of people here wouldn't bother to consider. Where I came from a car was a natural progression in life. If you could afford one, you had one. Having faced the humbling effects of our downsizing, my wife and I had become clear that more isn't always better. However, given the nature of the development we are involved in and the complexity of driving our son to a school in a nearby town 20 minutes away, not having two cars was becoming a problem. With me as a CEO building a new wellness center, event facility, and residential community of 400 homes, and my wife as our retail director and manager of several projects, there were just too many meetings, day trips, and changing schedules for each of us to not have a quick way to get around. In our minds, another car was the only answer.

Much like we would have in the United States, we began our research, looking for the most fuel-efficient, easily serviced, affordable, and safest car we could find. As partners in a new business, our income was mostly in the future. In the present we had just enough to get by each month, and some months not even that. We couldn't shop for style—price was the first concern. As the search continued, Monica and I noticed that our old habits had neither died nor completely disappeared. Like an innate and well-practiced instinct, we watched every car on the road, picking colors, makes, and models over and over in our minds.

With great fortune, Benjamin, our company founder and president, agreed to help us finance a car;

and the accounting office did all the work buying, insuring, and registering the vehicle for us. Sadly, the impulse to consume does not die easily. In the several weeks it took for our team to organize and complete the purchase, we could only think like spoiled children: *Why is this taking so long? It is so much easier at home in the U.S. We aren't even getting our first choice in color—it's unfair!*

Most people are aware that the problems of "those who have" are small compared to the problems of "those who have not." Most people profess to have power over what they own and need in life. The harsh truth is that the willingness to have less is much easier said than done for much of the world today. Many people today espouse values that they are reluctant to demonstrate or test—until life demands it. Even the impulse to develop and advance in countries around the world is largely fueled by a desire to compete and consume and not a desire to create peace or meaning.

It is embarrassing to admit but the release and loss of our house and belongings hadn't fully driven home the lessons of letting go in our minds, but the shame of being fixated on our car in a region where most people will never own one did.

Strangely, our car lease was the final test of our materialism. Where I grew up, and more so in U.S.

cities like Los Angeles, a car is an extension of a person's identity. In a world where people work too much and don't have enough meaningful time with family and friends, a car becomes an outlet for expression and a sense of self. Many people define themselves by their car, and feel defined by the car they can or must drive. All of this, naturally, is just a mythology, a totally false reality fed to us by auto companies and their marketing teams. Fortunately, the spell was broken, and we came to realize the true value of what he had. We now drive a car that says very little about us. It was affordable and it works for us. It's that simple. It is just a car.

Like the world community, the Riviera Maya is a region of extreme wealth and extreme poverty. Every day we are reminded to be grateful for what we have. Every day I remember not to take anything for granted—electricity, clean water, affordable fuel, anything. This magnificent place of natural beauty provides for us in ways that a big box store never will.

Less Is More

My awareness of consumption has dramatically changed since we have moved here. When we have little spending money for events or local attractions, we just go to the beach. When we cannot find the ideal products or snack at the grocery store, we rely more on fresh fruits and vegetables. When we cannot find the clothing or furniture selection we want, we just do without.

I went to a networking event for "green" businesses recently in Boulder, Colorado. I was feeling very timid when I arrived because our standards at Tao Inspired Living are very good and on the rise, but are not yet as squeaky clean as we would like them to be. The number of ecologically sensitive products in our region is more limited than you might find if you were building a resort in Colorado, British Columbia, or California. So, I was feeling intimidated by all the "green" companies and individuals that I was keeping company with.

My attention was on high alert and at each turn I wondered if my home life and corporate progress was really as green as it could be. As the event progressed and I added up all the new and alternative products I would have to buy to "green" my life, I came to a powerful personal realization: most green products today are simply replacements for conventional products, or they are new products to add to an already over-saturated home. Improving the ecological impact of a product is an important step, but the motive of many of these green companies is still to sell something. The goal is still material consumption, and a lot of it.

Since moving "south," I realize that what the world needs more of is *less*. By shopping less, spending less, and wasting less, we have a far better environmental footprint than when we used to go to the Whole Foods Market and purchase a green version of every excessive body care, snack food, and gourmet item we could dream of. Here by the Caribbean Sea we eat fresh, unprocessed food and only buy the toys and tools for living that are most important, rather than the ones that are most convenient. Living in the jungle or by the ocean you realize that the more you have, the more you have to tend to. Nature wears heavily on things here, and it's wonderfully so. It teaches us daily and keeps things in perspective. Life feels simpler, lighter, and, in the end, better for our planet.

Looking at what we learned from our move and relocation I now regularly ask myself questions that I believe would be helpful to anyone: *What do I really need to own? What if all I could have in life had to fit in the trunk of a car—what would I keep? What do I need more of? What do I need less of? What do I want, but can truly live without?*

Time for a Walk

Since we gave in to our desire for a second car, we recognize that a car is a privilage that comes with a cost. The first is to the earth. Regardless of the science on global warming, one clear fact is that the dependance on fossil fuels and the perpetuation of the pollution that results from them is just not a positive thing for the future of our world. The second cost is personal. When we drive more than we walk, we lose an intimacy with life. The beauty and wisdom of walking has been a tremendous gift of our move.

If you want to know a place better, explore it on foot. If you want to connect with nature better, do so on foot. If you want to know yourself deeply, spend time walking—not shopping, running, or talking . . . just walking.

On our street a quiet walk reveals the stages of growth that each plant creates and moves through. A walk helps us to know the climate and the seasons within a day. A walk is a way to meet people and sense the energy of life. Driving, like having too much stuff, is a focused form of distraction that feels justified in the moment, but causes you to lose half the story.

Three Tropical Teachings

1. *Simplify radically.* Reduce what you have, give away what you don't use, and then give away more. Remove clutter regularly.

2. *Walk more!* Get to know the world around you without technology or tools. Taste, touch, and feel firsthand. Drive less, walk more. At home, sit less, walk more.

3. *Focus on being not buying.* Your character is what needs attention, not your local shops. It is more important to focus on the qualities of your life, such as how you treat others and how you manage disappointment or challenges, instead of on the things you have or what you want to own. Shop less, and make more at home. Learn to cook with real ingredients, not with only those that come from cans, bottles, and boxes. Encourage your children to explore and experiment with their environment, rather than be handed their ideas and interests by plastic toys and TV shows. When in doubt, don't buy more.

Chapter Three

A KISS ON THE CHEEK

The Relativity of Time

I will never forget one of the very first lessons I received in Mexico. It was also one of my first days in the office at Tao. After a few days of settling into our neighborhood and exploring the area, it was time for a meeting with Benjamin, my new business partner and the founder of Tao Inspired Living. I arrived at the lobby of a partner hotel where I was to meet him and called him on his cell phone to let him know I was there. Benjamin was excited to hear from me and told me that he was on his way.

I sat in a large open-air lounge, watching the people and lizards pass by. The fresh sea air mixed with the warm humidity of the jungle and abundant flowers, and I thought, *Now this is my kind of place to have a meeting.* From the oversized lobby chair, I could see the ocean and the sun sparkling across its shifting surface. It was a lovely day, and I was feeling relaxed about our first formal meeting. Benjamin and I had met a lot over the phone and I had already made a few trips to visit the area, but this was really our starting point.

Some time passed, and I wondered where Benjamin was. I'm not normally impatient, but he was clear that he only had to leave the meeting he was in and stop by an office to pick something up, and then he would be right with me. Benjamin is anything but distracted and was always prompt at our meetings in the past. So as the clock ticked, I became more frustrated.

How long could leaving a meeting and picking up a piece of paper possibly take? Finally, I decided that I would move on and make the most of my day—maybe Benjamin ran into some trouble and maybe I could get away with a quick dip in the pool and head home. I was eager to have more time to play and explore the area with my son.

Just as I got up to go, there was Benjamin. "Hola, my friend!" he said, smiling. "Where are you going?"

"Well, I thought you got caught up in something else, so I was about to leave."

"No, no!" he assured me. "It's as I said—I left my meeting and grabbed something from an office on the way here. I came right away. You were leaving?"

Right away? I wondered. It didn't seem like the right time to get into an accounting of the minutes or to demand an explanation of how something so simple could have taken him so long. I had heard of people being on "tropical time," but it just didn't add up.

As we walked and talked about our work together, Benjamin mentioned there was a person he wanted to introduce me to at the hotel before I headed home. As was typical of the people I knew who lived in big cities and had "big jobs," I immediately and automatically calculated the time this event should take and when I would get home, already fantasizing about how best to enjoy the end of the day with my family. I was having a hard time staying in the present, as I was ready to go.

Then we walked into the next office and it happened. I saw it all clearly! The mystery had been solved.

When we walked into the room, there were three women sitting at open desks and a couple of men standing and discussing something. Benjamin not only introduced me to them all, but with each gentleman he exchanged a long series of handshakes and greetings, inquiries and jokes. Then with each woman, a kiss on the cheek and a similar series of exchanges. I wondered if maybe these people had just returned from a long trip, or maybe he hadn't seen them for some time.

At this point an interior office door opened and three men came out from a meeting with the manager we had come to visit. Two of the men knew Benjamin and the third was quickly introduced. With each interaction, the long chain of handshakes and questions and laughs ensued. They passed together through another closed door to meet elsewhere.

The room grew quiet, and we took a seat in a small waiting area, and waited. Five minutes later the three men appeared again, and on their way to the exit, they repeated the entire process again! This time it was farewells and good wishes, and more handshakes, shoulder slaps, smiles. This is how *every* meeting followed for the rest of the afternoon. In my corporate experience of the past, a nod of the head or a passing, "hi-how-are-you" was more than enough to acknowledge someone in a busy office setting. Naturally, my time calculation was completely unrealistic and I didn't get home when expected, but I knew that I had learned something important. It wasn't just about greetings—a handshake, a kiss on the cheek—it was about people.

Relationships Matter

Mexico has a reputation for being a country where people do not matter, as news shows and Hollywood films often portray it as a place where labor and life are cheap. With a massive and ever-growing population and a complex history of colonization, social unrest, and recent drug-related violence, it isn't hard to understand why this idea of low human value is common. However, once Monica and I settled into our new surroundings, we saw something very different. Most people who have lived or traveled in Mexico extensively will tell you the same thing. Here, relationships are the heart of life. Not only did we feel safe as newcomers, but we felt that our family was safer than ever before. Where we live, greetings are full and engaged, and people care about the answer. There is a basic joy in a daily greeting and acknowledgment. It's not just a formality; it's an affirmation that relationships do matter.

Here, we stop, we touch, we look each other in the eyes. We greet first with "¡Buenos días!" and then inquire, "¿Cómo estás?" I've experienced similar styles of greetings in many other cultures and places I have lived and traveled. In Native American communities, for example, the handshakes, jokes, and greetings are so essential that they could take up half the time of any encounter. In the villages where I stayed in southern Africa, I found that just learning the local greetings and exchange of inquiries and well wishes was enough to make friends for life.

What these and other cultures have in common is the awareness of the fact that we need each other—that life arises from relationships. When we forget we are connected, we forget ourselves. When we forget to acknowledge our friends, neighbors, and those who help and serve us every day, then we turn people into obstacles and numbers.

The Power of Community

Through my years of study and experience in the world of health and wellness, I have learned to be very intentional about how I discuss well-being. Still, many people think of health as a purely physical matter, one in which people, lifestyles, and places are easily interchanged. In my work and, for example, at our Tao wellness center and residential community, we have a clear focus on health, but we prefer to call it "total well-being." This expression is intended to recognize and affirm that health is more than physical and that true vitality has a holistic, integrated foundation. Well-being and wellness come from the inside out, and that means a focus on relationships. In addition to all the tools and teachings we offer, our goal is to help restore the most fundamental element of well-being: *connection.* This is why we, like many health and healing groups today, are doing more than just sharing information—we are building community.

Of course, connection begins with the self, includes our family, then spirals outward to include friends and local community; our natural world; our global community; and, in the end, Spirit, God, or a Higher Power—however you know it. Each of these connections is maintained as a relationship, with compassion, time, respect, dedication, humor, humility, and the willingness to love and be loved. Without relationships and connection, health is really a losing race, but with clear and joyful relationships, health is a natural journey that is always ready to be supported.

Relationships matter at work, at home, and even at play. The most effective people in the world are typically a part of the most effective teams. Think of your favorite athlete or musician or the most powerful CEO

41

or celebrity. No matter how individualistic their work may seem, they all have managers, coaches, assistants, families, fans, clients, directors, and collaborators who make them who they are. Oprah would have never succeeded with a team of poor producers; Bill Gates would have gotten nowhere if he had to create every new program by himself. The examples are endless.

Real Connections

The opposite is also true. People who become too isolated and unaware of the importance of connection—whether it's a stay-at-home parent or a famous actor—typically fall into an inspiration deficit, struggling to find balance and energy. Through my work with thousands of people either in groups or one-on-one, it has become very clear that loneliness and a lack of connection and community may be at the heart of more stress, illness, and imbalance than most realize.

The surge of interest in online social networking reflects this. People want to feel connected—all the time! Yet with all its gifts and advantages, things like Facebook cannot replace a real friend, a walk on the beach with a family member, or the power of looking into someone's eyes. Online connections play a valuable role in the world today, but we must be careful that they do not replace face-to-face communication. A helpful metaphor is health-food snack bars—those protein or energy bars we eat on the go. Snack bars are like online relationships: they are a great replacement for a missed meal and a super solution for a day without enough calories or nutrition, but they will eventually make you sick if it's all you eat. There is no substitute for real food. Virtual relationships have a power and a place, but don't let them replace real people and real time spent together.

The ability to connect and build community is a skill that is quickly on the decline. Looking around at how people function in this region shows an alternative to disconnection. Part of the time I spent writing this book was at a small boutique hotel in Tulum. Cabanas La Luna was managed by a friend of mine named Jacob, and I had the luxury of writing there because they were closed for renovations (thank you, Jacob!). I found a nice table in the shade where I could write with a view of the beach and Caribbean Sea.

All over the property, local men and women were working from the morning until dark. Thatched palapa roofs were being replaced, guest rooms were being cleaned, and repairs were being made everywhere. At some point each morning and afternoon, the clamor of the renovations would come to a halt. The entire team of workers would gather at the largest of the restaurant tables where a communal meal was served, which appeared to have been brought from home by someone. The tone of the conversation was typically light: people chatting or softly laughing, as it was a restful time away from work. Looking at the scene, you would not think of this as a lunch among co-workers—it appeared to be a meal among friends or family. Clearly not everyone in this group knew each other well, or even liked each other. But as I studied the event, I could see that there was a shared intention to enjoy the process and show kindness to one another at the table.

Later I watched the same people, now back at work: climbing roofs, digging trenches for cables, and sharing in other tasks. The tone of the meal seemed to influence the relationships on the job. Everyone appeared to work together with ease, forgiveness, and patience. I asked Jacob about it, and he affirmed my conclusions. "It's a very unique work ethic in this part of the world. People work very hard, but they also know to pace themselves, to keep relationships calm. They seem to remember that they are not totally defined by what they do, which somehow makes them better at it." I agreed, and it is what we've seen in our community as well.

Naturally, these are stories of ideal moments and places. Conflict and gossip exist in every workplace or community. This is not a pure utopia, and people are still very human. Nevertheless, there is a forgiving quality and a willingness to be kind, and a genuine sense of humor that is usually close at hand. People play soccer and swim together here; they eat together; they sing and worship and party together. The men and women of this region understand that life is not made up of rules, corporations, and wealth, but moments shared together—with all that it means to be human. It's the simple things that bring us together.

The culture of the region is very much influenced by the Mayan people, mixed with the special imprint of the immigrants. In tropical Mexico, nearly everyone is here because they want to be here. People have come from all over the world—Italy, Argentina, Canada, the U.S., France, Scotland, and everywhere else you can think of—and they do so because of an interest in quality of life. Much of the foreign population is made of accomplished individuals who simply had the presence of mind not to postpone their golden years and instead accept a more modest career in exchange for an extraordinary quality of life. This means that even the nonlocal locals—like my family and myself—have a natural desire to connect with like-minded people in a spirit of openness. It's not perfect all the time, but then again, nowhere is. Wherever you live, taking the time to build community is an investment that will give back a hundredfold.

Three Tropical Teachings

1. *Take time out together.* Make time for friends and family, and don't delay promises to get together. Make the time you do have into quality time. Spend time with the people you care about and need in your life, and clearly and regularly let them know you love and value them. Too often we expect the people we love the most to be okay with waiting for meaningful time together. Don't wait.

2. *Always acknowledge.* Greet people everywhere. Be helpful and present with strangers. Thank others for the little things and show appreciation for people in service roles. Even individuals you struggle with are likely doing their best; connect by first appreciating their role or effort, which can go a long way.

3. *Forgive (again and again).* When there is distress or imbalance in a relationship, start with forgiveness. Once you decide to forgive, you can then name the issue, face it, and heal it together. Don't wait long to begin. Remember

that forgiveness starts as a choice, not a
feeling. Forgiveness is as much for you as it is
for the one you are forgiving—or even more
so. It is the first step to freedom.

Chapter Four

SUNBURN AND SNORKELING

Too Much of a Good Thing

As I write this, my day-to-day office is located on the property of a large, all-inclusive hotel. Recently, as I headed back to my desk after a lunch appointment, I had to cross through the pool area, which is a coconut's throw from the magnificent turquoise sea. I often have the great fortune and frequent horror of seeing hundreds of tourists in their bathing suits. As I picked my way discreetly around the poolside, I couldn't help but notice the unabashed surrender of those who lay inert in the sun on their towels and deck chairs—a chaotic array of shapes, races, and sizes scattered everywhere. The scene resembles the aftermath of chemical warfare, but if you view the same setting just right, it seems more like you have stepped into a massive religious experience.

Surveying the area with care, you will realize that these men and women have traveled thousands of miles, interrupted their lives and bank accounts, just to lie comatose in the sun—until some unexpected moment when a small child or a loud water-aerobics class will suddenly wake them with a splash. Only then will they realize just how long they have been asleep and just how scorched their skin has become. You can see the walking wounded at night in the dining areas: red skin against summer dresses and T-shirts; pale white raccoon patterns around the eyes of those who at least remembered to wear sunglasses. It is natural to see this and wonder: *What were they thinking?*

Why the sunburn? Why travel so far just to sleep the day away? Why do we do it to ourselves over and over, always swearing that we will never do it again, and then we proceed to do so, again? It's not about the glamour of showing off our physiques. People sunbathe regardless of shape or size—with some at risk of being ogled, and others at risk of being pushed into the sea by a team of marine conservationists. All are equal beneath the great solar light, and we persist and insist. Despite the threat of skin cancer, a few unstoppable forces prevail, and here is where we find the tropical lessons.

Buddha and the Beach

The first reality check we receive when we visit or live in tropical places is that the rest of the world spends too much time inside. Even people who like to stay active often go to gyms, indoor swimming pools or courts, and recreation centers. Everyone else is typically in an office, store, car, or home of some kind. In the tropics stores, schools, and even work often takes place outside or at least in open-air settings. Our Tao residential community is filled with homes in which the outdoor living space is just as important as the indoor one. It is something that too many people are lacking in the modern world.

The poolside paralysis goes beyond the need to be outside. Aside from a desperate need for fresh air and a warm and euphoric dose of vitamin D, much of the world today is just too busy and simply needs a rest.

Even those who have little to do seem very good at being busy. Places to go, people to see—so much to do and the demand to do it all instantly. Social media and the innovation in cell phones, "tablets," and computers ensure a planet full of hyper-informed, overconnected, under-engaged people with lots to do and not much time to do it. The climax of stress in our world today lies not in the business of our lives, but much worse, in the business of our minds. A busy mind is an exhausting companion to live with.

A deck chair beside a pool or a towel on a beach provides a fantastic remedy for this modern illness. Doing nothing is one of the best things a person can do on a tropical vacation. Even after seeing all the ruins and visiting all the parks, many travelers' fondest memory of their stay is the days in which they did nothing at all! *Nothing.* People cross the planet to do nothing in a tropical place. Some do nothing for a whole week or more!

The commitment to solar hibernate is a greater leap than it seems. It's astonishing when you consider the typical attention span and need for entertainment at home. To do nothing is a radical act. When I talk to vacationers and those who return again and again to the area, I hear the same message over and over again: "This is the place where I finally get to slow down, do nothing, be nothing, and worry about nothing." After more than 20 years studying spiritual mysticism, I can assure you that this is not the talk of a lazy tourist. "Do nothing, be nothing" is the wisdom of the sages. It is the ancient aspiration of the most enlightened. A cool margarita, a swim in the ocean, and a perfect blue sky will transform nearly anyone into the Buddha. It may be fleeting, but it's hard to argue with that.

A Return to the Ocean

The longing to reconnect with nature explains more than sunburns; it also explains the swarms of people who make annual pilgrimages to the ocean. Because the Riviera Maya boasts some of the finest diving and snorkeling around the world's second largest coral reef, just about everyone who visits will make the time to don a set of rented snorkeling gear and swimming fins to catch a glimpse of a sea turtle or a rainbow-colored parrot fish. The coral wonderland is a short swim off the beach at any point, and individuals of all ages and abilities at least attempt to experience the curious and magical world under the sea. Like all things here, this childlike adventure is much more than it appears.

On a planet that is more than 70 percent ocean, a reconnection with the vast sea is a reconnection with our essence, our origin, and our sense of awe and vulnerability. It is scary, exciting, calming, and impossible to intellectually grasp. The mystery that is the ocean is as enchanting as the warmth of the sun, and it connects us to feelings that we rarely know how to access. On a tropical vacation we are unconsciously inspired to enter that mystery, and snorkeling is a popular way to do so.

Snorkeling isn't difficult, but it's one of those things that sounds much easier than it is. The process involves mouth breathing through a tube that sticks up above the water while you peer through a supposedly watertight lens pressed against your face so that you can "clearly" see what's going on beneath the surface. Much like the story of the emperor's new clothes, it's hard for a lot of people to admit how much water they swallowed or how often their mask was fogged up. But more important, when it is all over, few people recall any of the discomfort because one sighting of an eel, a manta ray, or an endangered green sea turtle is enough to erase all unpleasantness or reasons not to have tried it.

An explosion of color in a school of fish, and suddenly an hour of floating and seeing only shifting sands is made worthwhile. The ocean is our primal home, and time spent playing in her endless waves and massive presence is a universally healing experience.

It's a Jungle Out There

The jungle is another setting where visitors to our region step out of their normal routine and limits to explore and connect to something new. It's hard to imagine just how many ways you can experience the jungle in this part of the world. From tree-top zip-lines and cenote diving to jungle hikes, all-terrain 4x4 machines, ancient Mayan ruins, and monkey sanctuaries, there is something for everyone. The jungle provides some transformative lessons and those who take the time to explore her green and braided world are often surprised by what lies within the impenetrable walls of leaves and vines.

When I go beyond the perimeter, the first thing that always catches my attention is just how patterned and orderly the jungle is. Like many things in life, the complexity is impossible to understand from the outside, but from the inside, the roots and trails and layers are all revealed. The jungle reminds me not to jump to conclusions about people and situations; it shows me that just because I may not know the logic of an experience doesn't mean there isn't one there. What first appears as random and chaotic, is luscious, inviting, and restoring.

More than the rich beauty of the many shades of green, and the diversity of creatures present, the jungle also reminds us that Life is an unstoppable force. With enough light, warmth, and water, its plants, insects, and animals will consume anything. About 45 minutes from where I work at the Tao community is Coba, one of the largest "ruin" sites yet discovered, including one of the tallest Mayan structures.

When I first visited I was awestruck by the sophistication of the culture—the advanced design of the temples, roads, and homes. The human ingenuity and creativity was impressive, but the jungle showed a force much greater. In only 500 years or less, this massive development, stretching over 50 miles in width with towering pyramids, has been absorbed and almost completely hidden by the jungle. It is taking years to uncover just the smallest portion of an entire city!

Wherever organic life can assert itself, it does. In the jungle, you can witness how the power of diversity, opportunity, and symbiosis—growing interdependently —is truly an unstoppable force . . . even more so than humankind's ability to compete or conquer. Spend a day in the jungle with an open mind, and you will learn a lot about what it takes to thrive in the world.

The Ceremony of Life

One night I was invited to a Mayan ceremony called a *Temascal*. Much like a Native American sweat lodge, the Temascal is typically a small dome-shaped structure made of clay. The area is heated with stones that are brought in from an open fire and then steam is released as water is poured over them. Only somewhat like a sauna or steam room, the Temascal is usually much hotter and is always conducted in a natural setting. It is a very sacred ceremony of renewal and spiritual cleansing that must be viewed with respect and caution. There is nothing dangerous about a well-run Temascal; nevertheless, such traditions should never be played with or taken lightly.

The ceremony took place far into the jungle north of Akumal and lasted several hours in total. From the opening prayers by the fire to the different stages of the ceremony in which the door was opened and closed for fresh air to enter and more hot stones to be brought in, every step was done with care and reverence for the earth and spiritual world. This was not my first time taking part in a Temascal, and for me, entering the small structure is truly like entering the womb of the Earth, the belly of the Jungle. One of the gifts of this experience is the way in which it quiets the mind and creates a profound stillness and a feeling of openheartedness.

I will never forget the peace and bliss I felt afterward. Exhausted and deeply relaxed, I lay on the bare earth, looking up through the high jungle canopy to the dark ocean of stars floating above. In that moment of vulnerability, I couldn't have felt more nurtured. The sounds of the jungle were hypnotic, the fragrance intoxicating, and the stillness calming. The jungle is anything but a scary place; it's certainly not the tangled, treacherous mess portrayed in the movies. It is the home to thousands of medicines and food plants. It is a sanctuary unlike any we can create with our tools or technology.

The jungle floor is much more like a garden, filled with a range of textures and smells. The tall trees are like the columns of a great temple, wrapped with decorative vines and lifting up the high canopy of massive leaves and intricate branches, which is home to a colorful world of birds, flowers, monkeys, and reptiles. The rain forests and jungles are also the fundamental agents that purify the air and provide clean oxygen for the planet. Our Tao center and community is nestled in the jungle, and our residents and visitors say again and again that it has an unspeakable energy. Once you've felt that connection, it is hard to live without it.

Three Tropical Teachings

1. *Do nothing.* The great Taoist masters called it "wu wei" the art of doing by not doing. This is not about watching TV or going to a bar; it's about finding places and moments where your body and mind can simply rest without any activity or demand at all. It is about learning to unplug every day, even if it's brief. I knew a CEO of a major American company who blocked 15 minutes every afternoon to close his eyes and rest— nothing more or less. Many of the nurses and doctors I have worked with over the years also do something similar. Instead of gossiping, eating junk food, or texting on their short breaks, they choose to slow down and do nothing at all. Even when facing a pressing deadline, sometimes a short break doing nothing will give you the perspective and resilience that will ensure your success.

2. *Get wet or get dirty.* Staying connected to nature is not just about going to parks and zoos. Don't mistake a Sunday drive in the countryside for a deeper connection to the natural world. Any step is a good one, but

make a serious commitment to directly encounter the natural world through an activity that engages you without barriers or distance. Take a walk in the park, go for a hike, canoe, surf, snorkel, garden, or ski. Do whatever gets you outside that also allows you to experience the natural world without stress or competition. Don't wait for the right weather. Get outside often.

3. *Look after your mother!* Despite the awesome power of the natural world, humankind has the ability to impact water levels, weather systems, air quality, and the life span and population size of species unlike ever before in history. Don't just accept the gifts of the natural world; find a way to give back. Keeping local water systems pollution free, helping stray animals, being an advocate for political policy change, picking up litter, and learning to be a conscious consumer are all things you can do to be a steward of the earth.

Chapter Five

CATCH OF THE DAY

The Best Diet for You

After dropping my son off at preschool one morning recently, I stopped at a little café to eat a small breakfast and pick up a fast-food lunch for later in the day. Here "fast food" is very different from what is typical where I came from in Canada or in the U.S. Driving slowly through Tulum's colorful single main street of dive shops, tour operators, taco stands, souvenir stores, and merchants for the local population, I looked for a place that was both open and inviting. Beneath one of the many tall old trees that the main street was built around, I found my "diner" of the day.

First of all, at this food stop, there is no drive-through, so instead, I had to get out of my car and sit among other people who were enjoying their morning coffee, reading the newspaper, or watching the migrating travelers over their breakfast plates. There are no drive-throughs anywhere in Tulum—no one can imagine being in that much of a hurry! The café I chose was open air, so there was no glass window to hide behind. The decor was simple and unexpected: cheery green paint on the walls and beautiful old wood tables.

My quick breakfast was a *licuado* (also known as a "smoothie"), an amazingly inexpensive, popular, and common item here. Despite how hip and healthy the "new" modern juice and smoothie franchises are in major cities today, most tropical parts of Mexico have had a love affair with freshly juiced vegetables and fruits for decades, even centuries in some areas.

On our 3,000-mile drive to Akumal from Tucson, my father-in-law, Randy, and I once stopped in a tiny town near Tequila just after sunrise. There on the cobblestone streets in the old town plaza of Magdalena, we began our day with a hearty serving of freshly cut mango and a tall glass of newly made beet, carrot, and orange juice—which may not sound as fantastically good-tasting and good for you as it really is. All this and no additives, no preservatives, no frozen fruit, and no Jamba Juice in sight (and all that natural goodness for less than two dollars).

The "fast-food lunch" I ordered didn't take long to be served. Aside from the container, it looked nothing like fast food. Two fish tacos in corn tortillas, a serving of salad on the side, spicy pickled veggies, and fresh pico de gallo salsa (diced, fresh raw tomatoes, onions, cilantro, and an assortment of peppers, depending on the cook's preference). I asked what the fish was, and the man had to check. "I never know," he replied in Spanish. "We use whatever my brother has caught." This is what *fast food* should be like everywhere.

If you take the time to learn about the basics of a healthy diet for longevity, weight loss, and prevention, you will find that this well-priced taco stand was offering your doctor's dream meal. A little omega-3 enhanced protein, lots of fresh vegetables, some fermented foods (the pickled veggies are very good for you), and of course the fiber-full grains in the rice, beans, and corn tortillas. Nothing was fried and no added sugars or excess of salt. Grabbing a meal on the go doesn't have to be a compromise. Nutrition and the impact of your diet on your body and mind is a choice. I knew I needed something fast and on the go, but I also knew that what I was eating was fresh and health-promoting.

Fresh Living

I loved living in the USA and am a proud U.S. legal resident. I am also a deeply patriotic Canadian and love my homeland more than I can say. The Riviera Maya, however, has become one of my most favorite places on Earth. My personal passion (if it's not obvious) is holistic health, spirituality, and growing both through my relationship to nature. In the United States and Canada, the health and spirituality "movements" are large and growing. They are big business, and you can find healthy choices everywhere. Sadly, those choices are typically the more costly options, and they also tend to be located in places that don't always feel accessible to everyone. Here the essential ingredients for healthy living—such as fresh, local, and diverse fruits and vegetables, as well as locally raised meats like chicken and fish—are all easy to find and not too costly.

A healthier lifestyle is not as complicated as it may sound. Gym memberships help, personal trainers and nutritionists help, and therapists and doctors help. If you can afford it or find it, getting help and coaching is invaluable. Our Tao Wellness Center offers people access to these things because we want our community to have the very best and more. The reality, however, is that so much of what makes life fresh and vital in the jungles of the Yucatán is simple, low cost, or free.

To promote physical well-being and healing, most people simply need to *eat less* and *move more*—and do both *more often*. A diet doesn't need to be a typical diet, but a new relationship to the quality of foods you consume. Focus on what is as naturally occurring and simply produced as possible; and choose foods that are free of additives, preservatives, and chemicals you can't pronounce. Also avoid foods that are very high in fat, salt, and sugar. That's not hard to remember. Think of it in this way: the more steps your dinner is away from what it looked like growing in the field, the less healthful it likely is. This means fresh orange juice instead of a soda, fresh fish instead of a hamburger, and fresh-cut vegetables in a little salt and lime as an appetizer instead of a bag of chips with dip. It means going for a walk, playing a sport, or taking a swim in the ocean—not another trip to the movies.

Our little village of Akumal has a small monthly art show where a local business has dedicated itself to serving as a place for artists to stay on creative retreats and exhibit their completed work. Since we tend to be a community of active, interested people, most of our residents will make an appearance. When I look around on gallery nights, I see individuals of all ages, from teens to octogenarians. Mostly what I observe are people who appear fit, sun-kissed, in good humor, and relaxed in their pace. When I survey the room, I recognize the couple who walks on the beach *every* morning, the yoga teachers and local students, the scuba divers, the kiteboarders, and those who love to explore the ruins of the ancient cities and temples in the jungle.

Good health doesn't have to come in a bottle, a prescription, or from a high-end store. Don't ever let anyone convince you of that. It can come from easy changes—a little at a time. The bigger challenge for most people is finding a network of friends and family members who will support their new goals and habits.

In most cases you will have to start building your own wellness community where you live. A simple trick? Start with an activity you love, and then find others who want to do or learn how to do the same thing. Common interests are an old standby when it comes to finding like-minded friends, whether it's running, yoga, painting, kayaking, basketball, or Reiki energy healing. Your religious community can also help you find supportive, empowering individuals to meet with.

The Music of Life

Clearly life in the tropics is different than life elsewhere in the world. Having grown up in a place where winter often lasted more than five months of the year and decorum and politeness were prized qualities, a full relocation can be wonderfully jarring at times. The best example can be found at the local grocery stores. For some reason, every grocery store here from the larger corner store to anything bigger than a 7-Eleven plays the loudest dance music imaginable at the entrance to their store—and frequently inside as well! One of our local supermarkets even has a DJ that sits modestly through the *entire day* playing top forty dance hits and Mexican pop music for all who pass by. To me, it is amazingly strange, but incredible. Frequently people—tourists and locals alike—will have small fits of dancing, toe tapping, or head bobbing, as if the national epidemic was *dance*. Tour boats, ferries, and buses as well all play music—usually loud, often with a few people dancing in the aisles.

Naturally, you don't see people dancing everywhere, but the music serves as a reference point and reminder that at most local parties and events, dancing is only a short step away. From Mexico to Jamaica and from Brazil to Cuba, you will find that the opportunity and the need to dance will follow you like a spirit, waiting for your embrace. Though as with anything, dancing is easy enough to avoid here, it's also impossible not to be aware of the opportunity. As it turns out, leading physicians recommend dance as a significant health-promoting activity that aids in everything from weight loss, to longevity and stress management, to the prevention of Alzheimer's. Rhythm, movement, coordination, and pleasure are all critical activities that cause the body to produce reactions and chemicals in the brain and blood that are good for you! To get the benefits of dancing, you don't have to be a superstar or even a pretty sight, you just have to have fun and do it!

Fall in Love Again

Probably the best way people stay fit in this region of the world is by falling in love. I'm not referring to sex or love between two people, but falling in love with an activity or sport in which you engage and exercise your body. Not unlike where you live, people here do a wide range of things to stay fit. An advantage here is the diversity of practices, landscape, climate, and cost that are available—but I am sure you can find something you will love where you live.

Sit at the beach any weekend in Akumal, Playa del Carmen, or Tulum and you will see many ways people stay vibrant and fit, including (as I have already mentioned): kayaking, kiteboarding (check out **www .extremecontrol.net**), snorkeling, scuba diving, yoga, jogging, walking, and stand-up paddle.

Stand-up paddle?

Stand-up paddle is my new love. Some claim that it is an ancient Hawaiian sport and means of transportation; others are sure it's just a new fad. I don't care which is correct—it feels amazing and just right for me. Stand-up paddle involves standing upright on a floating board, much like a surfboard, and paddling with a long extended paddle. Some boards are as short as 9 feet, and some are as long as 16 feet ! Some boards are used on lakes and other flat bodies of water, and others on rivers. Some people do this as a means to catch waves and surf, which makes it a hybrid sport, allowing them to paddle toward waves in a standing position, rather than sitting and waiting for the waves to come to them.

As far as exercise goes, it is a fantastic workout much like cross-country skiing or swimming, engaging the whole body with a focus on balance and core strength. For me, this love isn't about what it does for me—it's about how it makes me feel. It's a "high" worth investing the time to find for yourself. The secret is to figure out which activity helps you feel like "you" again. Or even better, find something that helps you forget who you are all together.

Stand Up for Your Life

The first time I tried stand-up paddle was on the Tulum beach. I recall standing at the water's edge, uncertain of what I was stepping into yet eager to find out. The soft white sand beach stretched far to the north and south; the calm, iridescent turquoise water gently heaved and fell in front of me; and the sky shone with the light of the endless sea below. I was alone. At first it took some time for me to feel comfortable standing on the board with nothing but water all around. It was easier than I expected, and harder.

With my first dip of the paddle into the water I rushed forward. Because of my height and position above the water, I could see straight down, right to the sandy bottom. Four long silver fish darted past, as if they were only aware of the shadow of my being. I continued paddling, and a surge of exhilaration rush through me. It was only me and this thin board, gliding across the surface of the infinite face of water. Only sky above, only sea below. The merging colors of blue and green and white filled me with a calm vitality, a feeling that I never wanted to end.

Seabirds passed nearby and overhead, looking toward me as if wondering if I was really human, or maybe some part of their world that they had failed to notice before. I paddled onward, and flashing beneath me was a spotted ray searching the bottom for food. I saw shifting beds of seaweed, coral, and fish. I was slowly disappearing into the energy of the moment. It was no longer something I was "trying to do"—it was just happening. Everything was just happening, like wind or rain, like breathing. It felt like everything was moving together, and that I had stood up into a crack in reality that gave me a vantage point I had never imagined and yet fulfilled my dreams.

That is what it means to try something new and find yourself in an unlikely place. That is the gift of risk and openness. Health, fitness, and beneficial foods can be a celebration of life, not a function of the fear of death or a quest for contrived beauty. Exercise and mealtimes should not about numbers, but a full embrace of the miraculous gift of life that you have been given.

This is why people move here and begin their lives again. It is also something you can do anywhere, but you have to try. You have to step out into something new and discover what your heart is already connected to.

Three Tropical Teachings

1. *Eat fresh.* Eat lots of colorful fruits and vegetables. All foods you choose should be organic when possible, free of additives, locally grown as often as possible, and made by hand, with care, always! Your goal is to eat foods with as few ingredients as possible. Choose your proteins wisely, and ensure you have some with nearly every meal.

2. *Make your heart race!* For years, wellness authors have talked about the importance of getting active for 20 minutes a day. The simple truth, though hard to sell, is that if you really want health benefits, your exercise needs to be vigorous for a minimum of 20 minutes at least four times a week. Walks, golf, a game of tennis, or even a bike ride will rarely get your heart rate up if you aren't making an effort to perform at an intense level. Of course you should check with your doctor if you think this sounds dangerous for you. For most people, *not* getting their heart rate up regularly is more dangerous. Try new things, and find a sport or activity

you love. Whenever possible, make your
fitness fun!

3. *Turn up the music and dance.* What more
   can I say? In your living room, or at your local
   nightclub or YMCA, take time and make time
   to dance. Your comfort with your body will
   teach you something about your comfort with
   your life.

Chapter Six

HEAD IN THE SAND

The Stone Age?

It is often said and sometime sung, "You don't know what you've got till it's gone." When Monica and I left everything behind in the United States, the first thing we noticed, after the jaw-dropping beauty became less overwhelming, was how inconvenient certain things had become. Living in a little seaside town—which is less a village and more just a street with a handful of shops, restaurants, and villas—we found it difficult to obtain many items we normally took for granted, and we lost a lot of variety and choice when shopping. At first we didn't know anyone who could explain how things work and where to go to make life more familiar or easy. We didn't know what was normal or what was available. We didn't know if we had moved to the heart of the new era of modernity or to the Stone Age.

The beautiful little home we stayed in when we first arrived was like a magical cottage in the jungle. But there were often troubles with the water pressure and electricity. Our Internet signal only worked in certain rooms, and there were no glass windows or conventional air conditioning in the main living spaces, which was charming but difficult since we arrived when the humidity and heat was reaching its annual high point. We traveled a very rough road to get there, and given the overwhelming nature of complete relocation, we had the distorted idea that maybe everyone in the region lived like this. Maybe it didn't get better than this!

At first it was frustrating. We could no longer get our favorite treats like DVD rentals, toys, magazines . . . or more exotic items such as soy milk, healthy snack foods, or my favorite cookies from Trader Joe's. All these were small losses, but somehow they added up at a time when we really didn't know how we would fit in or if tropical life would work itself out for us. Eventually, we figured out where to shop for what we need, how to find the best of things, and ways to go without. As discussed in earlier chapters, we discovered that what we wanted and what we needed weren't the same. More important, we found that when we took the time to reconsider our needs, we were in fact in a place with an abundance of all we desired for a healthy, happy life.

But food wasn't the only difficult first step. Other things we took for granted—like cell phones, Internet access, cable TV, and even sending faxes—also took patience to sort out and organize. Over time we learned that all these things were available, and in our Tao community, for example, they are as easy to obtain as on a New York avenue. Yet when we first settled in Akumal, the infrastructure was just not as advanced, so we had to work a bit harder to achieve the luxuries of life. It helps to know someone with all the answers. We didn't. Nevertheless, all the delays and indirections have their advantages. During the time it took for us to negotiate payments and sign-ups to get ourselves technologically connected again, something magical occurred: *we* unplugged.

When we first arrived, we made the commitment not to rush toward re-creating our old life and comforts. We accepted what seemed like a step back from luxury and technology and the quick-fix life we knew. Instead of reaching for the familiar right away, we took the first five months to embrace the process of settling in. We simply let things like TV and the daily newspaper slip from our world. We wanted to be immersed in the people, the land, the creatures, the culture, and in our own experience of it all. It is not enough to live by the sea in a land of endless sunshine and mariachis if you are also holding on to a web of wires that blind and bind you. In the temporary absence of my BlackBerry (with three e-mail accounts!) and a constantly online iPad, I came to see that there are massive advantages to being disconnected, with your "head in the sand."

By the time we were fully unpacked and had organized the basic necessities, like our son's schooling, our daily work routine, and learning where and how to shop, we faced a major choice: what exactly would we *choose* to reconnect with? We had learned enough about the area and what is available from Cancun to Tulum, and it turns out that you can have just about anything! We weren't living in the Stone Age as we'd originally thought. After helping our Tao community members furnish and outfit their homes with decor and electronics, I was in shock at just how seamless the move from an American suburb to the jungles of Tulum and Akumal could be. We knew we wanted our community residents to have every option available, but did we want that for ourselves?

TV, News, and New Ideas

Without television, we became much more intentional about seeking news, and because we used the Internet, we found ourselves more engaged in the information we sought and were exposed to more diverse opinions and perspectives. Learning about the world became more like research and less like entertainment or a distraction. Also, without the presence of a TV, our nights and weekends were quieter, and we were more present with each other. We noticed that a home without television *feels* calmer in general. At night we often went for long walks together, or we'd sit at the beach, looking out for interesting shells and watching the shifting shades of color as the sun set.

Slowly our view of the world became more and more centered on our own experience and away from the experience and influence of marketing firms and materialism. We noticed that we could learn about the world without polarization—Democrat or Republican, right or wrong, hippie or sellout, rich or poor. We took each issue on its own terms and made decisions as individuals, and not as mindless members of some societal groupthink. Politics became more "gray," news became more global, and the biased opinions became more obvious.

Celebrity influence also disappeared from our lives. Suddenly my wife didn't care about what Kim Kardashian was doing; in fact, she just stopped thinking about her altogether. When we lived in Tucson, many evenings were spent turning our attention to what was going on with certain celebs, rather than what was going on with us. Narayan never watched much television when we had one, but he did watch small amounts, with unavoidably huge doses of advertising and product placement.

Now my son's framework for play is *not* cartoon characters, but the world he sees, invents, and imagines. Just the other night, he and I went for a walk together along our jungle back roads, and he made up a story that he told as we walked. His characters were the animals and creatures he is learning about here, and his stories were fascinating and developed with imagination and creativity provided by him alone—no mention of *Spider-Man* or even *Go, Diego, Go!*

There Is Nothing to Fear

During the summer of 2010, Tao signed on our Director of Communications: Jill, a well-known and loved PR specialist in the mind-body-spirit world of books and other products. When she accepted our offer, she (like me) faced the onslaught of questions and concerns from friends, family members, and colleagues: "What about hurricanes? What about the poor technology? What about the violence and drug lords?" Sharing the passion of our vision and being familiar with the region, Jill insisted that this was the right move for her and that the perceptions and fears of others were based on only a small sample of reality in Mexico, one that had nothing to do with where we are or what we are doing.

Continuing to work from the U.S., Jill then found herself in her own test of life. During July, August, and September of the same summer, the Riviera Maya underwent some of the most lovely and uninteresting weather: there were periods of extreme humidity and some exciting thunderstorms, but little else to speak of. Even a possible hurricane turned into a faintly qualified tropical storm. At the very same time in her home in New Jersey, Jill, on the other hand, endured a tornado, torrential rainstorms, flooding, an earthquake, near-hurricane conditions, and several days without power or Internet service on different occasions. The irony was not lost on her.

If those same things were reported from Mexico, the news headlines would have affirmed the evidence that there is much to fear and avoid south of the border. In contrast, the horrendous weather and disaster-like conditions that have haunted the U.S. in recent years are the focus of massive attention for brief moments, and then fade away as if they'd never occurred. The same is true of the U.S. news stories of mass shootings, gang and drug violence, and corruption in America. The stories are sensational, but fleeting, and somehow are never added up to suggest that the U.S. is a "bad place to live."

This story points to a powerful psychological fact that makes most people uncomfortable: our perception and focus shape our experiences as much or more than the things we are actually experiencing. We tend to turn feelings into facts and too often feel that our view and experience defines (or should define) the truth of others. Most often we pay more attention to the story-teller and filters and not the message.

From a spiritual or postmodern perspective, you might say that life is basically neutral; and we place layers of meaning, assumptions, evaluations, and old emotions upon it. What one person sees as an offer of help, another sees as an intrusion; what one sees as kindness, another sees as flirting; what one sees as a waste of money, another sees as an investment in happiness.

It's All in Your Head

Writing this book has caused me to reexamine my experiences in Mexico. As I drive to work, walk the streets of Tulum, or meet people in Akumal, I ask myself, *Is my portrayal of life here accurate?* I see poverty and illness; I see miserable tourists and joyful locals, or miserable locals and joyful tourists. I see a myriad of examples that give credence to the *opposite* of what I experience and believe. So whose reality is correct? Naturally, there is no one truth in the evaluation of a life or a place. I see things with my heart, with an eye for the spiritual lessons, and keep a positive attitude that seeks to connect and learn; and this place is rich and fertile ground for such a way of being in the world. It's a choice. Attitude and focus are a daily choice. If you don't make the decision, your history and need for comfort will make the choice for you.

Life cannot be reduced to the interplay of thoughts. There is energy, emotion, and other people, places, and things that shape each and every experience.

Nevertheless, our minds and what we take in define us. Most of us do not see what we are looking *at*, but what we are looking *through*. What does your lens look like? Do you see opportunity or uncertainty? Do you see fear or adventure? In the shopping mall the hungry person sees all the things to eat, the lovers see all the things to gift and share, the children see all that is new and fun, and the money conscious see all that is a bargain. Depending on the day or the moment, you could change your lens on life a hundred different ways.

One of the keys to finding paradise lies not in moving to beautiful places and living among supportive people; it lies in learning how to find, create, and recognize those things where you are right now. Inspiration is a way of being—not a place.

Look Again

Part of the joy of living in tropical places like the Riviera Maya is the diversity of people who move here: all walks of life and all cultures and beliefs. It helps as a constant reminder that life is not what we think it is. Life simply *is*, and we think our way around it.

When facing challenges of any kind, I suggest you try the following exercise, which you can do by yourself or with a friend (more fun). I, like many therapists, refer to it as "retelling the story." Take a situation you struggle with, and then imagine five new versions of how the story might be seen or told.

For example, I recommend retelling the story through the eyes of:

1. Another person

2. A person you know and respect

3. A famous wise person you admire

4. An inanimate object in the environment of the story (a chair, car, coffee cup, and so on)

5. A star in the sky, watching over your experience day and night

It may sound like an odd exercise, but people who live in inspiration are typically adept at choosing where to place their attention and what to tune their attention to. Try it . . . you may learn something.

Three Tropical Teachings

1. *Go on a media fast.* Try a total fast from the news media for at least a week; do this every few months. When you return to the news world, be more intentional and discerning.

2. *Take a techno diet.* Try a total fast from some or all of the technology that runs your life, such as two days without a phone or a week without the computer. Ideally, you should find a place with *no* technology to retreat to a couple of times a year, even if it is only for a day or two.

3. *Don't jump to conclusions.* Ask more questions, and consider other viewpoints. Decide as a whole person, and not as a role, a reaction, or according to a preconceived group opinion. Beware of judgments and generalizations.

Chapter Seven

A GOAT IN THE BACKSEAT OF A VOLKSWAGEN

Expect the Unexpected

It was another sunny afternoon in the Riviera Maya. I was driving through the town of Tulum midday to run some errands. I watched the usual mix of Mayan faces and frames, relocated Mexicans, and "expats" of all kinds wandering the streets. In flip-flops and dress shoes, straw hats and sunglasses, a diverse assortment of people merge and move through this fascinating little town. The architecture is quite forgettable, the streets poorly organized, and too many roadsides are not very clean. It never bothers me much though, and most of the time I don't even notice these imperfections, because the magic is in the rainbow of people and lifestyles that flow in and out of each day.

Look carefully and your eye will catch a maze of objects and oddities in any moment: yoga mats, woven baskets, Mayan art, colored hammocks, stray dogs, taco stands, tourist traps, and milk crates tied to scooters filled with anything and everything that will fit. It is the fullness of life without shame, and there is some special value in that.

I was still taking in the very unassuming diversity of the scene when I arrived at a red light, and an old light blue Volkswagen "Bug" pulled up beside me. Listening to music and thinking of my day, I didn't notice anything unusual about the rusty car until it pulled forward when the light turned green, and suddenly a large goat stuck its head out the back window. Two people in the front, and a large goat in the back! It was so unexpected, for a moment I felt like I was dreaming; and then realizing I wasn't, I couldn't help but laugh out loud. This is the gift of Caribbean Mexico: *Never get too comfortable, and always expect the unexpected.* These are good lessons no matter where you live.

Every country and region in the world has its own unique way of doing things. Here, we have "local time," which doesn't just mean "late," it means "when we are ready." There is a focus on *timing* not *time*. This difference can be difficult for many visitors who value and are used to punctuality. Not everyone runs late here; that's an exaggeration. Like anywhere, some people tend to be late and some tend to be on time. What is universal is the need to hold your expectations lightly and stay adaptable. Time is just one example.

My office presents a few other good examples of this lesson. Benjamin, my business partner, is the lead developer of a number of real-estate developments; and the most recent, prior to Tao, was the amazingly successful and beautiful golf resort and spa Sian Ka'an at Gran Bahia Principe in Akumal. At one point recently, Tao moved our offices into a new space. We were given a "start date" to move in and under Benjamin's lead, the new space was finished beautifully, with the exception of a few key things—doors, phones, chairs, and a table for the meeting room (which quickly became a storage closet). This was not a comfortable delay for me. It began to frustrate me as I wondered, *How could a team that builds entire hotels and residential communities—on time and on budget—not successfully move into an office!?*

I contacted our head administrator and explained that I needed a phone as soon as possible and that the wait was holding up my work. I received a prompt reply and was promised a phone by the end of the day. Sure enough, first thing the next morning I found a phone, brand-new, ready and waiting. I also received an e-mail confirming the new phone's arrival and wishing me well. Only one small detail was missing: there was no active phone line! I had my phone, but it was useless.

The phone line, like much in the office, was slow to get up and running. I had asked for a phone, but not a phone line; I had asked for a meeting room, but not a table to hold meetings. When expectations were not clear, results were not clear. We also had a woman who came three times a week to clean our new office, but each time she failed to throw out the trash or clean any surfaces (tables, windows, desks, and so on). She always showed up promptly and swept the area well. In fact, she was very sweet and kind, but until we actually asked her to clean specific things in specific ways, she typically spent a couple of hours each visit doing little actual cleaning. The things that I assumed to be obvious were not obvious here. The things that I expected were not expected here—not unless I asked.

What Creates Success?

This in no way suggests that projects are not successful or well run—quite the opposite! That is the mystery of Mexico, and many of our lives. This is the significance of Benjamin's role in the office story. While the little details that were needed to make our office function effectively were missing for what seemed like an endless time, Benjamin was busy building a brand-new lobby and over 200 new rooms for a hotel client of his *in less than a year* and was absolutely on schedule. His progress in development is celebrated, and efficiency like his is uncommon in the world of construction and development. The coordination, sophistication, and very fine final product have been a marvel to all. The irony is that the same team that built an entire hotel in less than a year (and sold it out in the first month), also took six weeks to get a table into a meeting room—and the first one that showed up was too small and without chairs.

In the end, the office was completed and everything looked great and became organized. The lesson, aside from cultural differences in communication, was more about the impact of expectation, focus, and attachment. What we put all our attention on was always completed, what we made a priority was always a success. Knowing what is a priority is half the battle. This is true in the health and happiness pursuits of most people. I had to practice these lessons throughout the first phase of my work here at Tao. In building and designing the Tao center and community, there had been many obstacles and surprises. I soon noticed that my stress level with all manners of delay and disorganization was directly related to my level of expectation. Areas where I had little expectation could be delayed and I felt no grief, but areas where I had a high sense of expectation were very stressful if they did not go exactly as I had planned.

All this until, of course, I realized that *being clear about expectations is always important, and feeling overly attached to outcomes is never helpful.* To manage the difference between the two, having a sense of priorities makes all the difference in the world. Clearly, stress is the distance between where you are and where you think you should be. Practice being exactly where you are, and life gets easier. Success requires focus and follow-up, not stress and control.

What We Need More Of

Life here is unpredictable in many ways, and it is much more than the culture; it is part of the magic of whom and what lives here. Whether it was the baby octopus that swam up to the water's edge one night to greet us on an evening family walk, that one strange traffic light in Playa del Carmen that nobody ever seems to stop at (except tourists and me), or the incredible spider monkey rescue center we accidentally found hidden in the jungle 15 minutes from our home (**www .thejungleplace.com**), this is a land of surprises.

For instance, a perfectly functioning cell phone will suddenly give people the message that your line is not in service but then minutes later it returns to normal; and basic things, like what a grocery store will stock and where they keep it located, can change from day to day. People here don't expect predictability, and they understand that things are rarely what they seem. If you can overcome the need for absolute control, you'll find that when things are allowed to be free and changing, incredible opportunity shows up.

The diversity and flexibility in this region is actually a mark of its resilience. The most incredible systems in the world—from sophisticated computers to jazz bands to enduring ecosystems and species—all possess the same amazing qualities: they are adaptable, they take advantage of change, and they thrive on diversity, not singularity. Strong leaders, lasting companies, good parents, and lifelong lovers exhibit those traits. They learn that the only thing that doesn't change is the fact that everything changes. There is variety, creativity, and richness to how they define themselves and relate to their communities. The resilience of adaptable systems is exactly what we all need more of in the world today.

The earth spins quickly toward ecological collapse through deforestation, overpopulation, pollution of water supplies and the oceans, species extinction, and the overdependence on monocrops for food sources. Global warming is really a small matter compared to these proven problems. Political tensions seem to be growing as polarization is trying hard to take root. More rigidity and partisanship has led to more confusion and less success for everyone. Technology overconnects and overeducates without providing meaning or accountability. The future looks dim if you question the sustainability and sensibility of our current path of progress. In creativity and innovation we are sure to find a clear path to a good future for all.

More and more individuals are gathering around ageless teachings of wellness and spirituality. More and more people are gathering in the spirit of collaboration and new thought. Where will you stand? Will you take the lesson of adaptability and change, or will you hold to the old world and outdated ways of managing your power? In my paradise, flexibility is a greater asset than control, and cooperation is a more successful model than competition. These are the choices that not only make for happier people, but also a healthier world.

Learning to love your life is not intrinsically a selfish act or mission. When you tap deeply into a love of life, you naturally seek to protect and respect all that you love. Looking for paradise is only foolish if you think that anywhere will be perfect all the time. Paradise is anywhere you feel closest to the truth of who you are—soul, self, spirit. The question, as my friend Claudio says, is, "Where do you like yourself the most?" It is true that the pursuit of paradise can be a dangerous path of avoidance, especially if it comes from a place of not wanting to take ownership of the role and relationships you are in. But when your paradise is about affirming life and the gifts you came to give, it becomes the most important search of all. When love is the motivator—and not fear—there arises both a deep self-satisfaction and a desire to ensure that love and balance for others. When you love your life, it is easier to see all that is "good and true" in the world. The reasons for being a part of a healing change is not because it's a good idea or it's profitable; it is because deep in your heart you feel and know it's the right thing to do.

What my relocation has affirmed for me is the very critical balance between having a clear and passionate direction and maintaining a flexible and responsive approach to getting there. Qualities that were once thought of as weak or undesirable in relationships, health, and work are proving to be core characteristics of endurance and success. In a shifting economy where unemployment rates are climbing around the world, resilience and adaptability are among the very traits that distinguish the indispensible from the expendable. None of this is new, though—it's only a remembering of what the great sages and seers once taught. This is the path to paradise. This is the timeless way of nature, and it's the enlightened way of the tropics.

Three Tropical Teachings

1. *Be focused and flexible.* Being flexible is not about being unfocused or without purpose. It's about adaptability and responsiveness. Always work toward clarity in your goals and intentions; and when change comes, look for opportunity, look for lessons, and look for the chance to renew and re-create. Be creative, think differently, and release your need for control.

2. *Practice nonattachment.* Nonattachment is about releasing the emotional hooks you "attach" to the way you want things to be. Practicing nonattachment means that people, places, and things don't need to be "perfect" or as you expect them to be. In fact, you can learn to be quick to let go of agendas, emotional burdens, and judgments of others. The more unattached you are to an outcome, the more efficiently and clearly you can pursue it—without the limiting forces of anxiety and clinging to something. Nonattachment is very much about having a neutral attitude and an ability to accept things as they are. What you think in one

moment is a disappointment might become your greatest gift in another moment. Creative breakthrough and innovation often arise in times of setback or surprise.

3. *Be creative.* A simple ingredient to success and longevity is creativity. Be willing to not only learn about new ways of doing things, but try them out. Those who are committed to business success or personal growth know that life is an ever-changing and unreliable process that is so much greater than what we can control or predict. Expose yourself to new ideas and ways of problem solving or being in the world. Even pathways you would never choose will help you gain new insight.

Chapter Eight

BEAUTY EVERYWHERE

A Bad Day in Paradise

Not too long ago, I recall my wife and I had an early morning "getting ready for the day" argument, which is also known as the "neither of us got enough sleep, our son is not cooperating, everything that could go wrong does, and now we are running late" fight. Most couples have them. Not what you would expect from two holistic healers living in paradise, but it's normal and unavoidable from time to time if you are fully alive and in a relationship with another human being.

What we fought about really doesn't matter in this story, because it was pointless and neither of us was right nor wrong. I suppose we both were a bit thought-less, which is proof that even in paradise people can have bad days.

In the days before we acquired a second car, our morning routines were often the same. We all worked to be ready to leave the house at the same time together. Usually one of us would drop the other off at work and then carry on with our son to his lovely little school in the town of Tulum, 20 minutes away; and then, after dropping him off, would drive back to the same workplace.

That morning when we got in the car, the tension was still painfully strong. Each of us remained silent in a mixture of avoidance and an effort not to make mat-ters worse. Narayan wisely kept quiet as well and, ignor-ing us, began his daily job of searching for interesting creatures at the side of the road (exotic birds, monkeys, feral cats—we haven't yet seen a wild monkey in our neighborhood). Where we lived at the time, the road to the highway was one-third rain-ravaged dirt, one-third pothole-filled concrete, and one-third hand-built brick with massive speed bumps. This is how we began our careful and awkward drive into the day. It wasn't the first time we started a morning that way.

"Look, look!" my son exclaimed as a beautiful yellow and orange bird flew close past our windshield.

"Oh, wow!" we remarked, both surprised and impressed, but not enough to break the icy silence any further.

On we went. Back into the cold quiet, staring out the window.

Then we came to the place where we pass close to the beach and an exposed and magnificent ocean view. Would we keep the morning ritual of greeting the ocean as we passed? I thought, *Of course,* and so, as always, I greeted the sea.

"Good morning, ocean," I waved out the window.

Then the two other voices in the car agreed, "Good morning, ocean!"

We stopped for a moment and noted that the sea was calm that day. The gentle waves carefully changed color with each motion, rolling from blue to turquoise, pale green, and then breaking into white foam. It was hypnotic and beautiful, so beautiful.

Monica and I both sighed. I could feel the warmth between us growing, and the day felt brighter.

I continued to drive, when suddenly we saw a little coati (a very cute, odd-looking, half-monkey, half-raccoon weasel) run into the middle of the road.

It stopped as if to wonder if we might be the more unusual sight, and then he passed into the bushes and disappeared.

"Coati!" we all shouted, and then together laughed at the silly chorus. The rest of the drive was a pleasure.

Beauty Therapy

It is difficult to stay upset in the presence of beauty or to stay angry when you let go of what you are holding on to. It's also hard to be frustrated when you bring your attention fully to the present. Anger and frustration are emotions typically linked to the past or future, so when your mind and heart are in the *now,* the source of pain vanishes. There are always those who, despite this, try to hang on to their pain in order to fuel the thoughts and actions they want to justify.

Beauty has a power over us that is mythical and mystical. True beauty takes us out of our minds and into our hearts—or more so, into our souls. It's why we save up our money for a tropical vacation. It's why white sand beaches and turquoise ocean water beats out the YMCA swimming pool every time. And it's why it doesn't matter how cheap our hotel is, or what a bargain tour we are on, because beauty is beauty and we will cross the world for a moment of it . . . and we should.

The experience of beauty is deeply healing, spiritual, and a part of total well-being. Since the dawn of civilization, we see the marks of beauty. From the decoration of tools to the paintings on caves and body adornment, even our most primitive ancestors made beauty a priority for themselves and in their relationship to God and Nature. Temples, pyramids, tattoos, statues, costumes, tapestries, and transport, everything has always been designed for beauty. Aesthetic and design are the interface between our inner and outer worlds. Where there is beauty, there is energy, attention, and even safety. Not all favoritism of beauty is justified and not all images of beauty are healthy, but neither fact changes the reality that we are hardwired for beauty.

The most celebrated hospitals have integrated art and beauty into their caregiving spaces and lobbies, for instance, and the most popular spas and hotels are also committed to creating a beautiful environment. If beauty didn't matter, it wouldn't be a focus, but people *need* beauty; they want beauty and they will pay to be surrounded by it. Sadly, distorted ideas can lead people to self-destruct through plastic surgery, anorexia or other eating disorders, steroid use, or an obsession with wealth to fund the acquisition of beauty. Flip the pages of a magazine or the channels on a TV, and you will see that beauty is one of the core drivers in life. It is so essential, it's simply expected.

If this is true, how well does the modern world manage this impulse? Ask yourself, *How do I manage this impulse? When do I create beauty? When does my idea of beauty heal and when does it hurt?* Moving to the Mexican Caribbean has helped me acknowledge the value of beauty and just what a powerful force it is. I have written about the influence of materialism and media in this book and the need to overcome such "magic" in the pursuit of a healthier mind-set and lifestyle. When beauty is unrealistic and rejects the natural form, such as in the case of models in glossy magazines or "perfect 10" news anchors, its distortion must be recognized and managed. It's vital to realize that the path to an inspired life is built upon harnessing the power of beauty in your life and not being caught by it.

Beauty As a Way of Being

Like in many parts of the world, if you come and explore where I live, you will find that beauty is important for most people who move here, and I expect also for those born here. Driving along the hotel strip in Tulum, it's clear, however, that different ideas of beauty will always exist. Some places are more like campgrounds or castaway villages; others are five-star modern palaces, and more like elegant works of art. Walking the beach in the tropics, I notice that people feel more beautiful when they are around beauty. Here most people wear their bathing suits with pride and confidence regardless of how they might compare to others—it is a testament to what a change in settings will do for a person.

My wife and I have made beauty a priority in our lives, and we do so now more than ever. From where we've chosen to live, to daily details such as how we set the dinner table, how we care for our living space, and how we honor and take care of ourselves is all about inviting the healing energy of beauty into our lives. Beauty is not about consumption or materialism. It is not about what or how much you have; it's about what you do with it. From the oldest Buddhist masters I have met in northern India to the most remote healers in African villages, even these sages ensured that their surroundings and instruments of life were kept well, clean, and beautiful.

I have an "extended family" and a teacher we spend time with in a small village near the Zimbabwe border in South Africa. Most of the people there are very poor by any global standard, but their clay homes are stunningly beautiful—meticulously built, decorated, and looked after. A simple hut—with a cow dung and dirt floor, a bed, and nothing more inside—is still one of the most beautiful homes I have ever stayed in. The white round exterior was kept spotless, the cool, smooth floors were always swept and adorned with elegant designs. Love and pride were almost visible in every brick and pathway.

You can create your own vision of beauty wherever you are—at work or at home, traveling, or even in a prison cell. True beauty is about dignity, authenticity, and a celebration of life. True beauty is a feeling. The energy of life moves in the beauty we create.

Not the Same When They Return

The topic of beauty as a *feeling* and an *experience* reminds me of one of the funniest and most wonderful experiences I consistently have now that I live in the Riviera Maya: international travel. More specifically, the shocking difference I see in the tourists leaving the Cancun airport from those who are just arriving.

When the airplanes unload in Cancun, it's easy to see who is a visitor and who is a local. Most of the people disembarking look a bit stunned from traveling and finally arriving in an unfamiliar foreign location. For many, it can feel overwhelming at first, and this is mostly because they are exhausted and/or filled with the fears of well-meaning yet uninformed friends and family members about what might happen if they get in the wrong line or take the wrong airport shuttle. The fears that many people travel with are disorienting, which adds to the drama and even to their appearance.

Most people look like they need more than a vacation: they look like they need a six-month stay at a treatment facility for the detoxification from modern life! Regardless of race or social class, the profile is almost universal: worn out and dressed inappropriately for the climate; stiff and jerky in movement with darting eyes; and shoulders hunched with the imprint of too much computer time, desk sitting, or child rearing.

My favorite is the overly matched young married couple. Both a little out of shape and out of breath, they arrive at baggage claim with messy hair and backpacks that are half open, spilling travel gear and airplane snacks. They have overplanned yet are underprepared. They work too hard at home, and they usually look winded and red in the face by the time they hit "Customs." These people desperately need beauty. They work too much at home and try too hard in life. They need to see and immerse themselves in beauty; and most important, they need to feel beautiful. A jungle yoga class or a day at the beach will do a lot for these individuals.

One week later, the departure gates look quite different: it is all the same people, but the atmosphere has dramatically changed. Beauty is the first thing you notice. The women have traded travel pants for summer dresses; the men have acquired sandals, sunburns, and a swagger. They do everything in slow motion. They take their time getting on the plane, they sit closer together, and they look relaxed. They are adorned like exotic birds, often with new hair braids or silly souvenir hats, but they don't care. They *feel* beautiful. When you feel beautiful, naturally you are beautiful, because beauty is an energy. Beauty is more than looks and perfect design.

What you see on the flights out of Cancun are people who have not only embraced their beauty and the beauty of the natural world, but you can also see what that evokes within them: *peace, patience, and the ability to be fully present.* This assures me that beauty and mindfulness are forever linked.

The Beauty of Mindfulness

Sometime around 1819, the great poet and mystic John Keats wrote the following, which has been debated and meditated upon for generations: "'Beauty is truth, truth beauty,'—that is all / Ye know on earth, and all ye need to know." Like many wise masters, Keats knew that a genuine connection to life reveals beauty, and true beauty creates a connection to life. If I had to write the words differently, I might say:

A deep experience of beauty leads to
A mindful awareness of the present.
A deeply mindful experience of the present,
Leads to the awareness of beauty.

Mindfulness is a newer English term that is a translation of an Eastern philosophical concept. There are also words like "mindfulness" in Indigenous traditions. Mindfulness became more commonly used in the West during the humanistic psychology movement of the 1970s, but remains a favorite term of modern spiritual teachers. Prominent in modern Buddhism, mindfulness refers to a quality of awareness or the practice of bringing your full attention, without judgment, attachment, or distraction to whatever you are experiencing in the moment.

Mindfulness can be described as a calm awareness, being in the moment, or full self-awareness. Buddhist masters and Hindu saints taught that learning to be aware of present-moment experiences was essential to enlightenment and basic happiness. In the great traditions of the West, Christians, Muslims, and Jews have other but equal ideas for mindfulness; and they all point the same way: the presence of God can only enter when you (your ego and busy mind) get out of the way. Psychologists teach that mindfulness is an essential step to healing and personal growth, particularly on the path of changing behaviors and overcoming addictions. However you look at it, being mindful is one of the most important steps to an inspired life.

What Does It Look Like?

You could say that the Riviera Maya is full of people trying to be mindful and those who are succeeding. Mindfulness is a quality of attention you can apply to anything—attending church, playing with your child, cooking, doing yoga, lovemaking, painting, running, or walking. I try to live mindfully every day, as often as I can. Exercise or spending time in nature will trigger mindfulness for me, and at other times I make a choice to bring the quality of mindfulness to what I am doing.

One night recently, I took a walk though our Tao property. Being a short distance from the ocean and immersed in the jungle gives the community and wellness center a distinct energy and feeling of sanctuary that just cannot be felt beside the ever-moving sea. The ocean carries the energy of expansiveness, openness, and endlessness; while the jungle feels like the embrace of the earth, a collage of green shades and heights. It is tranquil yet strong and affirming. Our property is also close to a world-class golf course, and when you walk the trails and paths, you can move from wild jungle to carefully crafted landscapes in a matter of minutes. It's like a tour of the human love of nature, crossing from the unrestrained to the designed, and it is all beautiful. Different kinds of beauty for different kinds of people.

Appreciating the diversity of our setting, I wanted to take a walk to feel the energy of our project and the soul of the place. It was a little before dusk. I could feel the growing calm within the jungle as creatures settled down for the night. Insects seemed to be changing shifts, and birds called more sparingly, their songs more haunting and clear. The sunlight turned to a golden orange, and dripped like honey in the trees. I stopped and took a few deep breaths. I'd noticed that my breaths were short. I consciously slowed my breathing and closed my eyes for a moment just to be mindful of my body. I could feel perspiration on my skin. I could feel my heart beating. I could hear my breath. I didn't need to fix or judge or change anything. I just relaxed into the moment and noticed how my body and attention changed.

I opened my eyes and continued walking—not thinking of work or home, not trying to get anywhere. I just enjoyed my own movement. With each step, sounds became louder and the patterns on the road and earth became easier to see. In a mindful moment of open awareness, even a passing car seems to move within the rhythm of life. With each breath, each second, the world seemed to become more vibrant and alive, and I became less and less intrusive in my own experience. It was like I was floating.

I heard a sound in the bushes nearby. There was no reaction, fear, or excitement, but a calm joy as I looked to see what might be there. A frog? A bird? It was a coati. This fascinating mammal always seems so cartoonlike to me. This one was sniffing the ground, maybe searching for food. I stood, silent, watching. Then it came out from behind the green curtain of plants and grasses, and crossed right in front of me. I could see every detail of its face and claws, every moving hair. I could smell it. It walked as if it did not even see me, and I wondered if my absorption into the moment was somehow physical. Had my inner calm caused me to merge seamlessly with the quiet world around me? I'll never know, but the creature continued without a care.

When it left, I was awestruck by the beauty around me. Parked cars in the distance, homes, jungle, golf course, and even street signs . . . everything was like music to my soul. A stray golf ball lay beside the sidewalk. The small white sphere was like a planet to me, or a small moon. Its glossy color, its pure form. Everything was beautiful in that moment. Mindfulness reveals the beauty of life. The beauty of life awakens mindfulness, and I pray for that gift each day.

Three Tropical Teachings

1. *Seek beauty.* Surround yourself with people and places that have a positive impact on you. Create surroundings for yourself at work and at home that uplift you and show a conscious commitment to shape the energy around you with order, design, and feeling. Look for the inner beauty in people, and you will find that beauty is everywhere.

2. *Practice mindfulness.* Make a very intentional effort to bring an open-minded, present-moment quality of attention to everything you do. Begin with simple activities and expand outward from there. Instead of trying to have no thoughts or a clear mind, just practice paying attention to your senses and the details you observe. Pay less attention to your thoughts and stories about things. Just focus on what you are experiencing.

3. *Find a meditative practice.* Learning to meditate is not easily done, but is a skill that is not only good for your physical

health, but for your mental and emotional self as well. Meditation comes in many forms and I recommend finding a regular practice that you can do briefly every day to help you feel more balanced and present. These short sessions will support your mindfulness work throughout the day.

Chapter Nine

THE CALL AND THE COMMITMENT

The Voice of Change

Our move was totally unexpected and not in the life plan my wife and I had been crafting. Fortunately, it was based on an unanticipated job offer for us both, but unfortunately, it also took place at a time when the press about Mexico was nothing short of terrifying. Pushing past our fears, we decided to seize the opportunity and soon realized that the negative media images had proven to be the complete opposite of our experience. This has been the best change of our lives.

Astounding innovation, amazing happiness, and divine inspiration all seem to follow a similar logic: *they defy logic*. The greatest leap of your life will not be easily measured, and the greatest opportunity will likely not be easily predicted. Just when you think you know which way you are headed, be prepared for a complete turnaround! The greatest things you can create do not begin in your mind, but in your heart and soul. Of course, you have the option to resist the call to change. You can stay in the same lane you've been driving in for years. Even when massive change is thrust upon us, there is still the matter of choice. How will you respond? How will you adapt? Will you be open? Will you hear "the call"?

The call for change, as it was in my earlier story about my change in jobs, is rarely as exciting as a spiritual voice singing in your ear (although that is possible, too). Typically, the call begins quietly, almost imperceptibly. It starts with a hunch, a feeling, a loss of energy, a loss of connection. It is as if your life is suddenly not fitting or feeling right, despite what may appear to be true. Pay attention to the signs. If you find yourself thinking, *It is time for a change* or *I can't keep going on like this* or even *This [job, relationship, city, or so on] doesn't reflect who I truly am,* then your innermost self—Life and All That Guides You—is trying to get your attention. A change is needed, a change awaits.

Knowing what that change needs to be is the next step and it is often not as clear as the first, which is simply recognizing the need for redirection. Consider this: I am someone who guides people through massive life changes. I recommend and strategize with them through these profound shifts, and I work on a deeply intuitive level. In other words, in much of my work, I rely on knowing unspoken things that I "sense" or see in individuals to help them gain fast awareness and transformation. Intuition is what has guided my life ever since I was a child. I am even prone to dream of things before they happen from time to time. I have also trained and worked as an executive business coach. Even with all these advantages and abilities, mastering my own change was not an effortless or perfectly clear process. I needed lots of help!

I talked to friends and had sessions with a coach. I consulted family members and mentors. I researched my options. I journalled about my desires and concerns, and tested and tried different options. Most important, I waited and remained patient. I took time every day to meditate, pray, and listen to what I was sensing and feeling. Ultimately, I realized this: *Creating* *an inspired life is not so much about manifesting what <u>you</u> want as it is learning to listen to what wants to be manifested <u>through</u> you.*

The Invisible Wall

The hardest step of magical and massive life change is the breaking of old ideas and assumptions. When people come to tour the Tao homes and Wellness Center, one of the most common points of resistance is not financial. "It all sounds too good to be true," we hear, "but do I really deserve this? My parents never had anything like this." We also hear similar comments such as, "I can't believe this is real. I've been hoping for something new and wanting to transform my current situation for years. Now my chance is here, I'm afraid to take it."

One client even said to me, "Everyone I know works so hard and suffers so much. Do I deserve this much happiness?" If you pay attention, you will notice that greatness and a truly incredible life aren't uncommon because the world lacks talent or people with dreams. They are uncommon because people have clear visions, dreams, and desires for a healthier life—but they are afraid to face change. Being fearful, needing permission, or holding on to old attitudes form the invisible wall that holds us back from our most incredible life.

The wonderful author, physician, and teacher Dr. Christiane Northrup is fond of an old saying: "If someone is stuck in the bottom of a deep hole, you really can't help by jumping in with them." It is the story of our society and our communities today. Disconnection, materialism, conflict, a preoccupation with false media, and an inability to invest in a lifestyle that is simple, happy, and health promoting are all too common. To create change, you need a vision to stay focused on, a path or practice to keep you centered. Think of a sailor at sea. He or she must navigate by what is fixed and adjust and adapt to what is changing. The wind, rain, and currents will shift and change day to day, but the distant shore and stars above remain unchanging in their place and pattern.

Having an open mind is critical in creating and adapting to change. In the United States, for example, millions of people are struggling to pay their bills and mortgages, and are also feeling dissatisfied in their overcrowded, fast-paced cities. Many of these individuals long for community, a better quality of life, and a closeness to nature and simpler things. The U.S. is full of smaller towns and rural cities that offer everything people are looking for. In nearly every state in the union, there are towns in desperate need of new residents and fresh talent. Recent decades of migration to big cities to pursue the promise of the American Dream has left many communities with a need for new family and friends. Why not you? Don't let your limited experience or thinking hold you back from exploring the unexpected and considering innovative options for your life.

Do You Have to Go Away to Be Inspired?

When the movie *Eat, Pray, Love* came out, which is based on the book of the same name, I was invited on a number of large syndicated and network talk shows to discuss whether inspiration only comes from traveling the world or if people can find it at home, too. As someone who wrote about my own world travels in *Return to The Sacred* and practical "stay home" paths to health and inspiration in *Inspiration Deficit Disorder,* many people were looking to me to settle the debate: Do you have to go away to be inspired? Is the grass really greener somewhere else?

The answer is complicated because both options have truth and possibility within them. Not everyone can or will be able to travel the world or relocate to a beautiful tropical destination. Can those same people find interesting, motivating, healing, and transformative choices where they live? Yes, absolutely.

Does it take an amazing amount of effort, focus, and commitment? Usually. The simple reality is that experiencing different routines and viewpoints, or living in an unfamiliar setting where the culture and landscape enrich you every day, has an incredibly powerful and irreplaceable effect. There is no way around that. To read about Zimbabwe and to spend a month there are just not comparable. Going to a day spa and standing waist deep in the Caribbean Sea are not the same; both can be relaxing, but stepping into the sea, like stepping into another world, presents you with an energy, a holism—a whole web of thoughts, feelings, smells, tastes, and insights—that you just can't fake or re-create with ease.

Living in another culture or region of the world for a week, or for a decade, is absolutely transforming if you go with an open mind and heart, and a soul that is willing to be touched by the energy of Life itself. When you see the world through the eyes of another culture, you are reminded just how relative and subjective life can be. Your way of life is nothing more than "your" personal, biased, and historically and locally built way of life. It is not right or wrong. It's just different. The snows of Alaska and the jungles of the Yucatán are nothing alike, but neither is "wrong." Each exists on its own terms in its own setting. In the same way, we as people often come to feel that what is familiar determines what is factual. We let our past experiences shape our choices and our vision of the future and, even worse, it shapes our view of the unknown.

Steve Jobs, the great innovator and founder of Apple computers, was known for his adventurous travels in places like India and other exotic locations where he explored the nature of consciousness and other ways of being in the world. Era-shaping leaders of the past, such as Alexander the Great, were educated and enchanted by their travels. Even great spiritual masters like Jesus Christ, Mohammed, and the Buddha were all known for their wandering, seeking, and exploring prior to their full enlightenment. Gandhi's near single-handed recovery of India from the British Empire was first inspired by a trip he made to South Africa. From Marco Polo to Oprah, and Queen Victoria to Neil Armstrong, you would be surprised by how much of the world has been shaped by people who have been shaped by their travel and experiences of other cultures.

The greatest lessons of my life have come from trying on and being invited into the lifestyles and worldviews of people far different from those I grew up with. I have stepped into experiences as diverse as herding sheep and sleeping in a small, round, wooden hogan on the Navajo reservation; to gathering medicinal plants with shamans and living in a northern village in South Africa that was far from paved roads or flushing toilets; to studying yoga day and night for six weeks in Dharamsala, India. Each experience revealed a new limit in my own thinking and helped me understand my own uniqueness and the universality of human nature.

Maybe not everyone can move into a new place, but with locations like our Tao community and the emptying of towns and villages around the world, the chance is more affordable than you'd think. When you consider that only approximately 35 percent of Americans have a valid passport, and that in other countries the percent is much lower, it is no wonder there is so much fear, racism, and disconnection throughout the world. Make it a priority to go see and experience the world—it's an amazing and beautiful place. Even if it's as simple as visiting the state or province next door.

The Commitment

In the end, whether we travel or stay home, whether we move to a new country or stick to the life we know, we are all faced with the power of choice in each and every moment. We cannot always choose what happens to us or how the world works, but we can make a commitment to how we intend to show up every day, and that is the most important part of living a healthy, inspired life. Living in the Mexican Caribbean is a thrilling gift, but it is easily overlooked. Locals, tourists, and expats like me and my family all have the ability to take our home for granted. It is easy to let a week or two go by without a visit to the jungle or the beach.

Wherever you live, you have to make your *total well-being* a daily promise to yourself. Your action, attitude, and accountability are all within your control. Total well-being comes from an alignment between who you feel you truly are and how you live and conduct yourself. The more clear and consistent you are, inside and out, the more vibrant your days will be.

Not long after I became the CEO of Tao Inspired Living, it became obvious to me that we must not only be absolutely clear about the experiences and opportunities we offer our residents and visitors, but we must also be absolutely clear and committed to those same core values as an organization in everything we do. Our health as a business, like the health of an individual, will thrive by virtue of our consistency, alignment, and clarity. If we commit to core values in all we do, there can be no mistake that those qualities will show up in the experiences of everyone we come into contact with.

To support ourselves and our clients in the pursuit of a vibrant, inspired life, our leadership team agreed to five key values. These five keys have come to be my own personal guideposts, and they may help you create an experience of total well-being. It is my most sincere belief that if you can embrace and commit yourself to these values, you too will find your own paradise.

Five Key Values of an Inspired Life

1. **Connection.** Connection is all about becoming aware of the importance of relationships. Relationships are the foundation of life. You are in relationship with yourself, your friends, family, community, other nations, our ecology, and a Higher Power. A commitment to connection is a commitment to maintaining these relationships in a meaningful and growing way. Connection is an ever-deepening process.

2. **Vitality.** Vitality is largely about energy and how you manage it in your life. Your energy is shaped by your level of fitness, the food you eat, and the energy of the people and places you encounter day to day. Your vitality is also a direct result of your clarity and feeling of connection to your life and purpose. Building,

protecting, and maintaining your energy in all forms is an endless life practice.

3. **Inspiration.** Inspiration is about seeking meaning, feeling a purpose, and cultivating a connection to the sense of inner peace from which energy and connection can flow. Inspiration is a result of deep listening and taking action based on the convergence of heart, mind, and soul. The things that inspire you shift and change over time, and so inspiration must also be questioned and explored again and again. Inspiration is the joyful voice of your intuition fully expressed!

4. **Service.** Service is both an attitude and a way of acting that feeds the totality of your well-being. Service is about giving of the self, helping others, being kind, and making a commitment to live free of violence and division. A giving attitude is something that will help you feel and maintain a sense of connection and purpose in the world. In giving we receive.

5. **Integrity.** Without integrity, your commitment to an inspired and vibrant life will be nothing

more than research, philosophy, and promises. Integrity is about being accountable and consistent. When we do as we say and say as we do, our inner and outer worlds match. With integrity, people will know your values by the way in which you treat others, the earth, and yourself. Integrity is not an invisible value; it is a clearly demonstrated quality that requires honesty, courage, and clarity.

As I come to writing the final words of this little book of lessons, I feel deep gratitude for the chance to share my story and some tools and teachings for a healthier life. I also know that you too have amazing wisdom and stories. When considering transformation and change, always begin from a place of celebrating who you truly are and all that you have accomplished—from the simple to the grand. The beauty of life ultimately lies within each of us. Beautiful people and places only help us to remember the truth of whom and what we are.

Outside, I hear the jungle birdsongs, laughter, and the sounds of an ancient language as a circle of Mayan friends gather to talk on the street nearby. Looking up, I see out my window to an endless expanse of rolling blue ocean and the diamond light that is scattered across the surface. Billowing, shining white clouds rise and swell in the far distance. I love my life. It is not perfect and it is frequently a challenge, but I choose it and enjoy it all I can.

It is not all as easy as it sounds. There is still much work to be done—more healing work ahead for me and for others, debts to pay off, aging loved ones, unknown setbacks, and a lifetime of responsibilities and choices that I will do my best to navigate and fulfill. I too have to break bad habits and manage my energy. I wrestle with my commitment to fitness and eating the right foods for my body. I will also face loss and illness and disappointment. Life won't always be easy, but it is possible to love something that can be difficult. Often the things that reward us the most require a lot of love, risk, and a great deal of hard work.

Building our Tao community is a project like that— a hard road, but a good one. Living here in this swirl of wild green forest, soft white sands, timeless monuments, and the radiant teal waters of Tulum, I have been taught some life-changing lessons. It is clear that despite how complex we make the world out to be, happiness and health are much simpler to achieve than we imagine. One deep breath at a time, one moment at a time, we can learn to love the life we have been given, in all its moments and stages.

Just as the ocean that stretches out before me is always different, always moving, and not always safe in stormy times, life too is ever changing; and if you know how to look at it, it is always, always beautiful. It's a worthwhile mission: create paradise wherever you are.

Three Tropical Teachings

1. *Get clear.* When you have a desired change, write it down as clearly as you can and find a person to help you to understand your choices. Review your goals with a counselor, a coach, or a friend. Another view will help.

2. *Know what matters.* Be sure that the foundation of your daily ambition is on building your character and the values you want to live by. A goal or dream life that is only about location, income, or romance is incomplete and will never feel fulfilling.

3. *Take a Simplicity Pledge.* Create a daily affirmation, prayer, or pledge to help you reconnect with your values and vision. The Christian Prayer of St. Francis, the Buddhist Heart Sutra, or a reading from the Tao Te Ching are all great examples of what you could easily read and meditate on. You might also review the five key values discussed in this chapter. Keep your pledge beside your bed or in your bathroom if you have to. You can also create one for yourself. Here's an example you can use:

My Simplicity Pledge

Today I am grateful for Life.

I feel grateful for all I am and everything that brought me to this moment, for in this moment I have a choice.

Today I will honor the people in my world, strange and familiar, and I choose to appreciate and co-create beauty in the world.

Today I will give more and be content with consuming and having less.

I will listen more and slow down often.

I will not indulge in what feels like unhealthy and destructive energy, and I will not contribute to such things by my actions or thoughts.

I will accept things as they are, and I will find the strength to make meaningful change.

My life and the health of the natural world are united, and my actions will reflect that.

Today I will enjoy the little things, and I will stay connected to Something Greater.

I will laugh more, say thank you more, and take time to enjoy myself and help others.

In this moment I am present, awake, and aware; and that is all I need to be at peace.

I am an inseparable part of God and everything in this universe.

This moment is enough to know that. This moment is all I need.

AN EXERCISE TO HELP YOU GET STARTED:
What Inspires You?

Most people know exactly what they love, what they need, and what they should do more (and less) of—they just don't do it. It feels good to read books and go to places that remind you of what you need and who you really are, because in the moment of connecting and fantasizing about the change, there is a brief period of euphoria and satisfaction that comes from the simple power of just thinking about what's good for you.

That is just how important being true to ourselves is—the mere thought of it makes us feel better. It's why we fantasize and even why we make promises we'll never keep. It's why we need tropical vacations. It's why we talk about getting together with friends and yet never do. It's why we set New Year's resolutions.

Sadly, for some people, it even defines their relationship to their doctor or counselor; they go again and again because the "idea" of wellness is so healing, but they never take action in between appointments.

Knowing what you want or need next in life is the easy part. If you think you don't know, set aside an afternoon and commit to the following exercise, and you will very quickly see how easy it is to uncover what inspires you. If it doesn't work, you can contact me for some personal tips on Facebook!

1. Set aside more time than you think you'll need for this exercise: Plan one whole afternoon for yourself and let people know you will *not* be available. If you can only manage a couple of hours alone, that will work, but more is better.

2. Make yourself a nice light lunch to kick off your time. Try something fresh, colorful, and not out of a can or box.

3. Allow yourself to rest or go for a walk after you eat.

4. Take time to do something you love that you don't do enough or at all anymore. You could see a movie, go fishing, visit an art gallery, read, "shoot some hoops"—whatever

you enjoy doing. It should be fun and "unproductive."

5.   After you've been fed in body and mind, create a quiet time and place to relax. Take out a piece of paper and a pen (try not to use a computer or electronic device of any kind for this).

6.   Try a deep breathing exercise. For example, for a full two minutes, take deep breaths in and out through your nose. Each time imagine that the air travels down into your belly, *instead* of puffing up your chest.

7.   Fantasize. Ask yourself, without any regard for limits of any kind: *What would I do? What are my talents? If I could do anything with my free time, what would I do? If I could do anything with my talent and interests, what would I do? If I could create any job doing anything, what would it be? What needs to change in my life? What inspires me and interests me—and why?*

8.   Write down your answers to each of these questions. Don't censor or edit. Just write freely, even in simple point form. Just brainstorm about what your heart longs for.

9. Circle all the words and actions that you can begin to choose or make happen right away.

10. Underline all the things you could create over time.

11. Place a star beside things that feel very unrealistic right now.

12. Go to a local printing or shipping and mail business, and make a few copies of your notes.

13. Create a plan to take action on what is within your control. Commit to two changes immediately, even if very small.

14. Review the limiting and unrealistic items with a coach, counselor, or a friend whom you view as an inspiring person and a good creative thinker.

15. Finally, imagine yourself in the new life you dreamed of, then create or envision the steps you've had to take to get there. Keep it simple and rewrite your vision clearly. Then plan in reverse, asking yourself what it would take to get there. Always plan your action steps, your attitude necessary, and how you will stay accountable. Then get started—without delay.

LEARN MORE

Would you like to learn more about the partnership between Hay House and the Tao Inspired Living? Explore our website at **www.taoinspiredliving.com/hayhouse**.

You can also sign up for news from the Tao center, updates on Dr. Ellerby's work, and our amazing calendar of world-class teachers and events at **hayhouse@taoinspiredliving.com**.

Are you interested in our inspired residential community? You can learn more about our property in person during an inspiring and wellness-focused Discovery Weekend, which includes a workshop with Jonathan Ellerby, Ph.D.; a choice of wellness classes; a Hay House gift pack; luxury accommodations; and all your food and drink for less than $100 a night. Find out more or sign up now by contacting **hayhousedw@taoinspiredliving.com**.

ACKNOWLEDGMENTS

As always, there are too many wonderful people to thank who have supported me in my life and work. For this particular book, I owe deep thanks to the founder and my partner at Tao, Benjamin Beja, and Hay House president Reid Tracy. Deep gratitude to the Tao team and Lucia for helping my family and me arrive and settle with ease.

Thank you to Jacob at Cabanas La Luna for his kindness and a magical place to write. Thank you to the team at Tan'Ik for always being a help and our new community. Much love and gratitude to Canyon Ranch and Jerry Cohen, Mel Zuckerman, and Carrie Kennedy for all the support and opportunity. Thank you to PR goddess Jill for being a great and ongoing part of my career and life. Thank you to Rachel, who helped me survive my last book and to launch so much of what I am doing now. Thank you, Ned Leavitt, for your friendship and professional guidance. Deep gratitude for the entire amazing Tao team for your hard work and dedication to our vision (with special thanks to Angelica for helping with this great book cover)—I am continually inspired by all of you!

Endless love and thanks to my mom, my dad, my brother, my sister, Brenda, Jess, and all my friends and family who have supported my growth and choices over the years. Infinite gratitude to my spiritual dad Gene Thin Elk for all you've taught me, and to the whole Wase Wakpa family for all the ways you've loved and supported me. To Mark Samuel, whom I still thank for many lessons in leadership, facilitation, and life, which I know are present in all I write. Thank you to my amazing and magical wife, Monica, for all you show and teach me. For my boy, my miracle, Narayan, thank you for being my teacher and for helping me learn so many of the great lessons of the Riviera Maya (in a fun way).

Thank you to the Ancestors of this sacred and magnificent place for bringing me here and helping us create the Tao community. My love and gratitude to the oceans, jungle, sky, and all natural forces here in the Akumal area. To the Divine Spirit of Life—the Oneness that is All and the only real Thing—I am in Gratitude, Connection, and Love because that is your essence, and may I remain aware of that every day of my life.

Thank you, dear reader, for giving your time to read my stories and hear my heart. Endless blessings to you, good luck, and . . . *adios!*

Love and blessings,
Jonathan

ABOUT THE AUTHOR

Jonathan Ellerby, Ph.D., is an important guide to inspired living in today's hectic world, bridging cultures and professional disciplines to help people find what works. Featured as an expert in film, print, television, and radio, Jonathan is the author of *Return to The Sacred* and *Inspiration Deficit Disorder,* and the CEO of Tao Inspired Living in the Riviera Maya of Mexico.

With a Ph.D. in comparative religion and over 20 years of experience in the fields of holistic healing, counseling, integrative medicine, and corporate consulting, Jonathan makes wellness practices and spirituality simple. Drawing from his travels around the world and experiences with healers from more than 40 cultural traditions, he focuses on what works to bring balance and inspiration to everyday life.

Website: **www.jonathanellerby.com**

We hope you enjoyed this Hay House book. If you'd like to receive our online catalog featuring additional information on Hay House books and products, or if you'd like to find out more about the Hay Foundation, please contact:

Hay House, Inc., P.O. Box 5100, Carlsbad, CA 92018-5100
(760) 431-7695 or (800) 654-5126
(760) 431-6948 (fax) or (800) 650-5115 (fax)
www.hayhouse.com® • **www.hayfoundation.org**

Published and distributed in Australia by: Hay House Australia Pty. Ltd., 18/36 Ralph St., Alexandria NSW 2015 • *Phone:* 612-9669-4299 • *Fax:* 612-9669-4144 • www.hayhouse.com.au

Published and distributed in the United Kingdom by: Hay House UK, Ltd., 292B Kensal Rd., London W10 5BE • *Phone:* 44-20-8962-1230 • *Fax:* 44-20-8962-1239 • www.hayhouse.co.uk

Published and distributed in the Republic of South Africa by: Hay House SA (Pty), Ltd., P.O. Box 990, Witkoppen 2068 • *Phone/Fax:* 27-11-467-8904 • www.hayhouse.co.za

Published in India by: Hay House Publishers India, Muskaan Complex, Plot No. 3, B-2, Vasant Kunj, New Delhi 110 070 • *Phone:* 91-11-4176-1620 • *Fax:* 91-11-4176-1630 • www.hayhouse.co.in

Distributed in Canada by: Raincoast, 9050 Shaughnessy St., Vancouver, B.C. V6P 6E5 • *Phone:* (604) 323-7100 • *Fax:* (604) 323-2600 • www.raincoast.com

Take Your Soul on a Vacation

Visit **www.HealYourLife.com®** to regroup, recharge, and reconnect with your own magnificence.
Featuring blogs, mind-body-spirit news, and life-changing wisdom from Louise Hay and friends.

Visit **www.HealYourLife.com** today!